by J. Schappet, A.Malkusak & L.D. Bruya

*high*EXPECTATIONS

Playgrounds for Children of All Abilities
Early Childhood Edition

First Edition
October 2003

Boundless Playgrounds® and the National Center for Boundless Playgrounds® are registered trademarks.
Velcro® is a registered trademark of Velcro USA Inc.

ISBN: 0-9746514-0-0
Printed in the United States of America

The National Center for Boundless Playgrounds
45 Wintonbury Avenue
Bloomfield, CT 06002 USA
(860) 243-8315
www.boundlessplaygrounds.org

dedication

We dedicate this book
to *all* children,
past, present, and future,
who learn about life while playing,
and to our families—the people
we really enjoy playing with!

contents

acknowledgements

AS THE TASK OF WRITING THIS FIRST BOOK HAS MOVED toward its close, we have thought with great thankfulness about the people who have helped to make this work fruitful.

In September of 2000, a knowledgeable group of people were invited by the National Program for Playground Safety, at the University of Northern Iowa, to participate in a conference to explore the characteristics of children and developmentally appropriate play on public playgrounds. During this conference, Larry and Jean interacted with some of our nation's brightest thinkers about the nature of child development and the characteristics of play. Within those few days, our thinking was influenced. No doubt, our resolve to write about observable play behaviors was emerging, as we clarified their benefits for all children. We would particularly like to express our gratitude to Rheta DeVries, Francis Wallach, Carl Gabbard and Greta Fein for your contributions to our thinking about children and their play, during this conference. Special thanks to Donna Thompson, Susan Hudson, and Donna Mokricky for organizing this significant event in the evolution of this text.

One colleague challenged our thinking and encouraged our work—Steve Langendorfer. We thank you for your friendship, concern for children and for reading our "stuff".

Our text has been immeasurably improved by the contributions of our editor, Nancy and our graphic designer, Tom. Thanks to both of you for making us sound and look our best.

Finally, we would like to acknowledge the contributions of the National Center for Boundless Playgrounds® team that worked on this project, that managed, that read and reread drafts, and that kept us on track. Thank you to Patty, Kristen, Thad, Ellen, Amy and Dianne for your commitment to get these thoughts down on paper and printed so that others can share in what we have learned.

Editor's Note: Jean Schappet, Tony Malkusak and Larry Bruya all came to understand by different routes the need for barrier-free, developmentally advantageous play environments and the fundamental necessity for this in children's lives. Their passion for their work, however, comes from the same place—their hearts.

from Jean Schappet

IT SEEMS IMPORTANT TO TELL HOW I GOT HERE. Since every journey begins with a first step, as a source of information, I want to describe the first steps on my journey toward developing playgrounds for children of all abilities.

Our family (my sister Nancy, her husband Bob, my husband Charlie and I) began building backyard playgrounds in the late 1970s. Our business started as a cottage industry—on a picnic table—then grew to more than 60 employees and a manufacturing facility. Early in our business we observed that when we built playgrounds that were good for children with disabilities, the equipment was better for all children.

As the designer of our products, I studied children's development and a wide range of childhood disabilities including cerebral palsy, pervasive developmental disorders, Down syndrome and sensory integration dysfunction. For more than two decades I studied kinesiology, brain development, child psychology and self-esteem, and early childhood pedagogy. I attended and presented at numerous conferences. Over time,

with the layering of all of these varied disciplines, pieces of an approach to children's play environments began to emerge. Clearly, outdoor play environments should provide more than just a place for children to "blow off excess energy." In fact, children do not have excess energy. They act differently outside because they are able to make choices, be in control, and find things to do that are interesting to them.

From all my studies and from years of observation, it was evident that all children benefit greatly when the play setting supports their current interests. Interesting places to play always hold children's attention the longest. But, what were the characteristics of the interesting places? And, did the characteristics of the interesting places to play need to change? I wanted to find a correlation between the type of play that attracted children and maintained their interest and play that provided long-term developmental benefits.

Our children grew up playing on the equipment we built. Our observations of their experiences and the experiences of other children on the play equipment guided our thinking about what children want in an interesting play environment. By the early 1990s, we had developed a backyard product line that encouraged changing the structure as children grew and a product line of public-use playground equipment.

During the mid-90s we built a playground for the UCP (United Cerebral Palsy) Center in Richmond, Virginia. This was a watershed project for our company. It was the first time that, in collaboration with knowledgeable professionals, we built an entire playground for children with severe and profound disabilities. Our enthusiasm for this project was surpassed by the excitement of the children who played independently in the "tree house" when the project was finished. One child even communicated for the first time as he waited for a turn on the swing. It was thrilling to hear the countless stories about children with disabilities playing and to know that they were also making developmental gains that had not been achieved through therapy alone. Here was yet another proof that when children play, profound things happen inside them.

I met Amy Jaffe Barzach as she was mid-process for Jonathan's Dream, a playground built in West Hartford, Connecticut, in 1996 as a memorial to her and her husband Peter's son, Jonathan. We talked one Saturday afternoon for an hour. We laughed and we cried. She asked me if I could help her clarify her vision of a "wheelchair–friendly" playground. I said I would be happy to help her.

After the playground opened, Amy treated me to a tour of Jonathan's Dream. I had found a soul mate. Amy and I had arrived at the same place but in completely different ways. We both realized that all children need to play, that all children need to play together and that public play places fill a unique void in the lives of all children, regardless of ability or disability.

When a 2" article about Jonathan's Dream appeared in *Time* magazine in December 1996, Amy's phone began to ring with calls from people all over the country. "Could you help us do what you have done?" Amy's tender heart could never say no and she asked me to help.

In 1997, our family sold our playground manufacturing business. It was time to start the next chapter of my life. Amy and I, as volunteers, and a passionate team of parents and professionals established Boundless Playgrounds® as a grassroots nonprofit organization that spring. In 1998, thanks to a generous three-year grant from Hasbro Children's Foundation, Boundless Playgrounds opened an office, hired staff, launched education and outreach programs, and was able to help 24 disadvantaged communities create playgrounds for their children of all abilities. Amy and I were following our hearts.

With 63 playgrounds complete at the start of 2004, the dream has only just begun. As a nonprofit organization, Boundless Playgrounds believes that barrier-free, developmentally advantageous play environments should be within reach of every child and that play environments should give children of all abilities a chance to play together, each at his or her highest level of ability. It is my hope that this book will bring us one step closer to that dream.

Jean

Jean Schappet is the co-founder & creative director of the National Center for Boundless Playgrounds. Jean began her career in the construction industry, but when her family started building residential play structures for children, her life began anew. She had found her passion and mission in life. During more than 25 years of designing play environments and specific use components, observing children during play, and studying available literature, she came to understand how simple changes in a play environment could vastly affect a child's opportunity to reach their full purpose and potential. She loves crafting play environments for all children, teaching and writing, and is a frequent speaker at regional and national conferences.

from Antonio C. Malkusak

WE ARE ALL SHAPED BY DEFINING MOMENTS IN our lives and by the choices we make. Some of these choices are easy, while others have a profound influence.

I was destined to be involved in the development of children's play environments. One of my first defining moments came when I was just nine years old. I fell from a set of monkey bars and hit my forehead on an asphalt surface below. Evidently, there were other plans for my life, so instead of becoming an injury statistic, I walked away from that fall with only an acorn-sized bump on my head.

When it came time for college, I knew exactly where I wanted to go and what I wanted to study. In 1985, my dream came true and I graduated from the University of Illinois with a degree in landscape architecture. I was ready to take on the world, and with two opportunities to choose from, it was my first defining moment professionally. One offer was from a golf course architect and the other, a landscape architect/park planner position, came from a gentleman named Ken Kutska with the Wheaton, IL Park District. I sensed a passion and energy from Ken in the work that he did and the community he served. The choice was an easy one; I became a "Parkie."

Ken was my first professional mentor, introducing me to other people in the profession and allowing me to grow and develop. He got me involved in playground safety and a program that was just starting through the National Recreation and Parks Association, or NRPA. In 1991, the first National Playground Safety Institute, or NPSI, was held in Baltimore, MD. I just **had** to go. Ken was one of the organizers and presenters, along with other prominent individuals in the field such as Deborah Tinsworth, Dr. Frances Wallach, Dr. Donna Thompson and Monty Christiansen. You could sense by the energy and the conversations these people were having that a movement was happening, and I was privileged to be there.

Less than one year after that first NPSI, my wife Diane, who had earned her Ph.D. in developmental biology, accepted an offer with Johns Hopkins University to do her postdoctoral fellowship. Ironically, we were headed back to Baltimore; this time it was going to be our home.

Our five and a half years in Baltimore were enjoyable and marked another defining point in my professional career. Though I had limited opportunities there in the parks and recreation field, I maintained my passion for playground safety and design and got involved in any way I could, regardless of the situation or circumstances. In 1995, I commuted from Baltimore to New Jersey to work with Bill Foelsch, executive director for the New Jersey Parks and Recreation Association, who was implementing an innovative playground safety awareness program for his parks and recreation agencies.

Under Bill's vision for spreading the word about playground safety, we conducted over 250 playground safety audits for more than 75 communities throughout the state. In 1998, Bill Foelsch and Ken Kutska asked me to join them as a member of the NPSI Executive Committee. Honored to be a part of that esteemed group, I accepted their gracious invitation. I still serve on that committee and have been one of the NPSI playground safety-training instructors since 1999.

Another defining moment in my life occurred in 1998. Diane completed her fellowship at Johns Hopkins and received three offers to be a professor and conduct research at the university level. She was fulfilling her dream. We decided to accept the opportunity from the University of Iowa, in part because with three young children (and a fourth on the way), we wanted to be closer to our families who resided in the Midwest.

Moving to Iowa proved to be one of the biggest blessings for me. Iowa, namely, the University of Northern Iowa, is the home of the National Program for Playground Safety, or NPPS. In 1999, I had the opportunity to attend one of its playground safety schools. This is where I first met Jean Schappet and Dr. Bruya (Larry), who were two of the instructors for the program, along with Dr. Donna Thompson and Dr. Susan Hudson. Jean and Larry's enthusiasm, passion, and commitment were so evident, I was naturally drawn to them. We had several long conversations into the night. Larry shared his insights and experience, and Jean discussed playground environments for children

of all abilities. It is hard to describe, but something was clicking between us. I just could not get enough of Jean and Larry.

A couple of months after the NPPS School, Jean called. We had a two-hour conversation and at the end, she asked me whether I was interested in working with her. I said, "In a New York minute."

In January 2001, I joined Jean and Amy Jaffe Barzach and the organization they founded, the National Center for Boundless Playgrounds. It has been my calling, ever since I was nine years old when I fell off those monkey bars.

Jean and Larry are incredible collaborators and mentors. They are truly inspirational and have challenged me in ways that I have never been before, to be the best I can possibly be. I hope that *High Expectations* inspires you to greater heights for children and play.

Antonio C. Malkusak became the director of design for Boundless Playgrounds after working as a landscape architect in the parks and recreation field. Tony received his bachelor's degree in landscape architecture from the University of Illinois in 1985. He has worked in two Illinois park districts, and as a landscape architect in Maryland and Iowa. During his life, Tony has spent many hours observing his children and other children during play. He uses these observations and his professional experience to propel forward the state of the art in the play environment industry.

from Lawrence D. Bruya

M Y THINKING STARTED WITH THIS: Billy Deidrick and I were coming in from sixth-grade recess. We were talking about the kids that didn't get it, or couldn't play because they weren't chosen. We decided to start a summer program to train kids so they could play better. We didn't know at that time that we didn't get "it".

Then in undergraduate school, I dropped out of coaching and went into early childhood and elementary physical education. I didn't like the fact that only certain children were selected to play. I was beginning to get "it".

I had the good sense to marry Lorna. She was an early childhood teacher, and she gave me perspective. With her help I was able to understand better.

Then, I was a principal in a school in the Alaskan bush. Our Eskimo children had no playground, so I set aside dollars to build one. The administrators overruled my budget changes and we lost the playground. The children still had no place to play. The administrators; they didn't get "it"!

So I went to graduate school and studied…and then studied some more. For one of my projects, I constructed a paper-and-pencil playground-assessment instrument. The

object was to assess the developmental appropriateness of the various play environments on the playground. Now, I was back on track and getting "it" again!

I teamed up with Steve Langendorfer, and we focused on development in children during play on equipment and in the water. We worked hard—all-niters spent studying. The hallways of Purdue probably still echo our dreams. For me, Steve was another Billy. Together, we got "it"! He helped me and I helped him— Michele Mersereau, too.

Then Peter Hixson and his family clicked with Lorna and my family. It was apple pie à la mode. Our children played together. Our wives hit it off. Peter and I could work, he in developmental language patterns and I in developmental motor patterns.

Purdue was "good years." There Peter and I designed and constructed the first indoor play center. We called it "the frame." It represented a major advancement in our thinking. Later, we installed one in a child-care center in Texas and another in a speech and hearing clinic in Nebraska. Preschool-age children with short attention spans played for 45 minutes. It was major, and we loved it…. Together, Peter and I were sure we got "it" now!

Lorna and I cleared out the living room in our house that first year at the University of North Texas and constructed a wooden-floor indoor play center/environment that became a meeting place for our preschool-age children and the neighborhood. Now our children were getting "it", too!

As my profession intensified, I got better at "it" and closer to my original mission formulated first with Billy, then Steve, then Peter, and always Lorna. The Committee on Play (AAH-PERD) undertook and published the first national study on the assessment of playgrounds. Curt Fowler and I started a small company to design and build playgrounds for young children. Work with Jay Beckwith and Carl Gabbard expanded my boundaries. Writing and researching led to the Timbercraft line designed with Nan Simpson.

Work with Donna Thompson and Susan Hudson encouraged me in playground supervision. Geoff Wood and I started a process for playground certification. I installed playgrounds with Glen Prosser. The career was blossoming and I was working hard to understand more—to really get "it"!

Then, I got luckier. I began teaching with Jean Schappet. It was like the door on understanding opening all over again. The dreams were just like Billy in '58, Steve in '74, Peter in '75, always Lorna, and now Jean in '95. What a great personal growth time…. Tony Malkusak was one of our students at first. That's how the three of us met. He was into and always dreamed of building great environments for children's play. "It" was in his blood. He was passionate.

Our philosophy on children's play environments and our writing about it came together. Jean and Amy Barzach, and others, established Boundless Playgrounds and the mission was set—foster and create barrier-free and developmentally advantageous playgrounds for children of all abilities. Tony became part of the Boundless Playgrounds team.

Here we are today with *High Expectations*, our first book together. Future texts are in the planning stages. Who would have dreamed? Let's see—first Billy, then Steve, Peter, always Lorna, Jean, and then Tony. "There but for the grace of God" is what I say. And I'm thankful to be alive and working with these good people, and for the children He loves.

So, my journey continues.

Lawrence D. Bruya, PhD, a professor at Washington State University (WSU), teaches in the College of Education, Movement Studies. Early in his career, Dr. Bruya worked as an elementary school physical education specialist and as a classroom teacher. While an associate professor at University of North Texas, Larry developed and directed a preschool and elementary school children's gymnasium and aquatics activity program. This helped him understand the affect of design and equipment selection on the play patterns of children. He has held positions of department chair and associate dean at WSU. He has written extensively about child development and playground design, and received several outstanding educator awards during his career. Dr. Bruya is a member of the Academic Advisory Board for the National Center for Boundless Playgrounds.

introduction

Life is full of simply amazing things. Two that have always fascinated the authors are bumblebees and children. Bumblebees aren't supposed to be able to fly—their wings are too small and their bodies are too heavy. Yet they fly! Children come into this world with nothing more than raw potential and pure determination to acquire all the information they need to learn. Yet they learn!

Bumblebees and children share another common trait—they are naturally attracted to what they need to thrive. Bees are attracted to pollen to make honey, and children are attracted to play. Play is truly dynamic in that it leads to huge developmental learning in children, regardless of ability or disability. Despite this, in too many cases, our society has failed to address the play needs of children with disabilities. This failure can be rectified by providing barrier-free, developmentally advantageous play environments, where children of all abilities can find fun things to do, interesting places to be, and everyone can be in the middle of play. Influencing the creation of playgrounds for all children—children with and without disabilities—has been the mission of the National Center for Boundless Playgrounds® since it was established in 1997.

Shaping the play environment and its setting to maximize the benefits that independent and self-directed play provides all children is a high calling—one that the authors and Boundless Playgrounds takes very seriously. For play, like no other activity in life, gives children the myriad of experiences they require for healthy development.

HOW CHILDREN PLAY IS THE FOCUS OF THIS BOOK, because what they do during play is fundamentally tied to the whole developmental sequence. By looking at what children do during various play behavior phases, the authors have isolated key factors that when present in a play environment, attract children to play and engage them in longer, more developmentally advantageous play episodes.

That children must achieve engagement during play is a major factor in the developmental usefulness of play. All children build the internal systems of their intellect during play—that's why where they play and what they can do during play are so important. Therefore, how play environments are configured and how they are facilitated for play makes a difference in the quality of play experiences that all children will have!

Boundless Playgrounds has undertaken the publication of this book to serve as a lay person's guide to the configuration of play environments and their facilitation. *High Expectations* is a book in two parts: this printed text and the attached CD. The CD titled *Toward Developmental Advantage: A Supporting Text for High Expectations* is an academic presentation of this material. References are provided to support each of the key points.

The ultimate goal is to revolutionize the way we think about public play spaces and the resources that are applied to providing children's play environments. *High Expectations, Early Childhood Edition* is the first of three books that will be published by *Boundless Playgrounds* about play environments for children of all abilities across all the stages of their development. This book is focused on play environments for the youngest and least sophisticated players—those children commonly referred to as preschoolers.

Above all, however, the authors hope to influence adult thinking about the importance of outdoor play and give direction for the creation of play environments where all children—with and without disabilities—can experience the true liberty and learning of play.

It is amazing—bumblebees to pollen and children to play, each able to do the impossible in spite of the improbable odds against them.

CHAPTER ONE

underlying ASSUMPTIONS

underlying ASSUMPTIONS

- *I really like children.*

- *I like to watch what they do, seeing what interests them.*

- *I like to listen to what they talk about, to themselves and to others.*

- *I like the things that they make, the choices of color, forms and materials.*

- *I like to study them as they make decisions, seeing all of the nuances of their choices.*

- *I like to observe as they deal with conflict, sometimes solely focused on their own benefit and sometimes moved with compassion for another child.*

- *I really like children.*

L IKING CHILDREN HAS LED TO MANY OPPORTUNITIES TO observe children, and through these observations, a few underlying assumptions about children and play have emerged. Underlying assumptions are very interesting because they are the foundation for our actions but are rarely given the honor of forthright discussion. Such is the case of our assumptions about childhood and play. The design of children's play environments and the preparations that adults make for the play adventures that take place there are telling about our beliefs of the importance of play in the lives of children.

To begin this text about play environment design and the relationship between childhood and play, it seems appropriate to straightforwardly present the underlying assumptions that have become the foundation of *High Expectations*. Believing that the observations that have led to these assumptions are true and universal, it is our hope that you will find children you know living in these pages.

assumption NUMBER 1 - *children are egocentric*

F ROM THE VERY EARLIEST CRIES OF A NEWBORN, children demand a response from their adult caregivers. They need food, warmth and freedom from discomfort. As they become more neurologically sophisticated, their perception of their needs is enhanced. They require input and they demand it. They are egocentric because they have a lot to learn and are very motivated to reach their objectives.

With the start of each day, it seems that they rededicate themselves to the pursuit of the very next, most important thing they need to advance their own development. Even the most experienced teachers are often surprised by the egocentric determination of a child.

Zoe was a bright, determined youngster of 2½ when she entered my Montessori classroom. From the beginning I knew she'd be special. She didn't race through the initial lessons as many of the new children do. Zoe enjoyed each new lesson and the inherent repetition that led her to perfect each task. She was so stubborn! She refused to be cajoled into doing things that went against her mindset at any given time. I swore that Zoe's dark eyes and curly hair grew darker and curlier with each stamp of her foot!

Zoe mastered many difficult tasks early in her Montessori life. She often asked for an introduction to a piece of apparatus that I felt was beyond her reach. Her ability to concentrate continually impressed me, so I cautiously guided her toward those requested tasks. I was not prepared, however, for Zoe's resolve to learn how to tie.

Individual fastening frames introduced the child to buttons, lacing, snaps, Velcro® closures, hooks/eyes and ties. Zoe quickly learned all of the basic frames and pestered me to introduce her to ties.

One snowy winter morning, the cold floor in my classroom took on new meaning for me. I decided to give Zoe a lesson on the tie frame. She watched as I brought the frame to a table, and she pulled up a chair to join me. She sat quietly by my side as I untied and tied each of the five bows on the frame. It was now Zoe's turn. I moved my chair to the side to give her some space. With her dark eyes growing bigger and bigger, Zoe untied each bow. As I coached from behind, Zoe finished the frame (with some frustration on her part, but no tears!). My introduction done, I was off in another direction, happy to let Zoe return the frame to its proper place on the shelf.

I next chose to sit on the floor (cold as it was!) to observe a child working on a mat with the red and blue number rods. Within a minute, Zoe was in my lap, the frame in front of her on the floor and her short, stocky fingers at the ties. Two and a half hours later, Zoe had made a permanent impression—and not only on my pants!!! She hopped off my lap with the last bow tied and put away the frame. Zoe's immediate "need" was to learn how to tie; her determination and her repetition led her to master the tie frame in one morning session. I knew she was delighted with her achievement, but what remains a mystery to me to this very day is whether or not Zoe knew that she was sitting in my lap the entire time!

While it is evident that Zoe was focused and determined, the underlying truth is that her need to learn how to tie on that day was far more important to her than anything else that was happening around her. Determination and focus are two of the observable behaviors in children because they are innately egocentric.

assumption NUMBER 2 - *children are compelled to play*

PLAY IS IMPORTANT IN THE LIVES OF CHILDREN BECAUSE in it, they direct the choices, make related discoveries and enjoy the benefits of being self-directed. The satisfaction gained from these experiences is compelling, and children seek to duplicate this pattern often. The connection between an object and its usefulness during play is the magic of play that adults often overlook. This is called engaged play.

When moving into engaged play, children isolate some concept they have formulated in their mind and couple that concept with something interesting that they have just discovered. This is one of the many ways that engaged play begins. It may appear that the child is still right next you, yet when you listen to what he is saying and watch what he is doing—that child has gone some place else in his imagination.

Once drawn into engaged play, children create a sphere around themselves where various things are used to fulfill aspects of the imaginary environment. For engaged play to happen, children must be at the core of the activity—not observers. They must be the primary initiator of the play event where they direct the outcome of the event.

It was a warm spring day in Iowa. I could sense it in the air; this Memorial Day weekend was going to be something special. Not only was it a three-day holiday weekend, but my mother and father were coming from Chicago to pay a visit. All week long the buzz around the house was that Papa and Noni are coming, Papa and Noni are coming! Prior to their arrival, we had several chores to take care of around the house. My wife Diane and oldest daughter Rachel, age 11, would clean inside while I led the outside clean-up with the help of my three other children, Darrell, age 7; Grace, age 4; and Katherine, age 1.

With little time before Papa and Noni were to arrive, I formulated a quick mental list of tasks: put toys away, prepare and plant flowers in the front yard; little Katherine was to use her tiny broom to sweep the sidewalk. My list set, we were ready to get started. Little did I know that Grace had her own list of things that she just <u>had</u> to do.

Our front yard is quite typical for homes built in the 1950s in the upper Midwest. Several mature trees line the streets, providing cool shade for pedestrians and for those who wish to relax on their front porches. The trees also provide a home to the many squirrels and birds that seem to enjoy entertaining my children at any opportunity. On this day, a robin was busily gathering items to make its nest while mourning doves sang their distinctive melody. It was a great day to be outside.

I was preparing an area in the front yard to plant brightly colored perennials. As I used the digging trowel to loosen the rich, black soil, I called for Darrell and Grace to help with the planting. Darrell was chomping at the bit to get his hands in the dirt and was on all fours in no time, but Grace was nowhere to be seen. Just then, she popped out from behind the trunk of a large maple tree, but she was not ready or interested in planting flowers.

Her plan for the morning did not include planting flowers with Dad and Darrell. As I observed, she collected seed helicopters that fell from the maple tree. She pranced all around our front yard, bending over to pick up these helicopters, and tucked them inside her shirt, which she folded up to create a little makeshift pouch. Darrell and I, amused by this sight, stopped to watch Grace do her thing. I noticed that she had this complete and utter focus, oblivious to everything around her. It seemed she just had to pick up those little helicopters.

As soon as Grace had filled her pouch, she ran over to our front porch to dispense the harvest. She then sat down, lined up the helicopter seeds in a long row and began to strip away all the outer coverings one by one until she had a pile of little green maple seeds. My curiosity now getting the better of me, I moved to get a closer look at what Grace had in store with those fresh green seeds.

As I approached, I heard Grace in conversation with herself. Speaking softly in that little four-year-old manner, she was saying, "Papa and Noni are coming and we need to make chicken nuggets for everyone to eat. I'll put them in the pot…."

I yelled to Diane. "Get the camera. Gracie's making chicken nuggets!"

My wife, confused by my comment, stuck her head out the door to see about the commotion. When she caught a glimpse of Grace making her feast, Diane let out an infectious laugh, the kind that a proud parent makes when their child does something special. Needless to say, she hurried to get the camera.

As all this was going on, Grace was still in her own little world, completely engaged in her play. She whisked by me, continuing her mission to get more "nuggets." Again in her soft voice, "Time to get more chicken nuggets. We need a lot. It's my favorite…."

Clearly, Grace had far more interesting things to do in the front yard than plant flowers. Her discovery of the maple tree seedpods gave her the very objects she needed for engaged play. Play is the vehicle for gathering and organizing experiences. Making food to feed others is an activity that is fascinating to young children, yet one that they are often excluded from in the real world—although they could be included in daily food preparations. Play is compelling because when a child is in charge, she can do all of the things that interest her.

assumption NUMBER 3 - children's play behaviors are age-related, not age-determined

ON ANY GIVEN DAY, WHAT A CHILD MAY DO DURING AN engaged play episode is governed by a few related factors: What did he do yesterday that was interesting? What does she have to play with today, and what play supports are offered in the surrounding area? It is common for children to use the same toys or play supports for a season of time. Each time the usage may be somewhat varied, but to engage in play, some of the factors must be known and others must be discovered.

Children use play behaviors to discover the things that they don't understand. Watch a child climb on top of an unfamiliar structure for the first time. He will use a prone posture climbing technique—both hands and feet in contact with the surface. As skill and familiarity come into place, he will use a more sophisticated climbing skill—at first a cross-lateral pattern, then feet only as a base of support with hands used to add balancing stability. This model is also true for children who are venturing into new areas of intellectual, social and ethical development.

Jonathan was an outside kind of kid and he liked to take his collection of die cast cars with him. The best thing about these cars is that they fit in the pockets of his little boy jeans. On any given day, he might have one stuffed in each pocket and one in each hand. At four years old, he appeared to be very interested in racing. In reality, he was interested in comparisons. Jonathan would assess what was bigger or smaller, what was older or younger, skinny or fat and most important, fast or slow. Jonathan's policeman father had a fast car with lots of lights and a radio. Fast cars were a very interesting consideration to Jonathan.

In the backyard Jonathan had a fort. This fort was four feet high and had a ladder to climb up and slide for going down. For nearly a year, Jonathan's favorite activity was to climb the ladder, sit down on the platform and go down the slide, around and around. Sometimes he slid down on his tummy, feet first. Other times he went head first, and when Mommy was watching closely, he went down sitting on his bottom. The slide was a great thing to use with a pile of leaves at the bottom to crash into in the fall, and in the summer, the sprinkler added a sense of coolness and adventure.

But now it wasn't so much fun to just go down the slide. The cars were new and far more interesting. He liked the way they zoomed on the floor in the kitchen, but they wouldn't roll at all on the carpet in the family room. When you play by yourself, it's hard to have a race. Every day Jonathan looked for places to play with his cars.

Finally, one day, his mother let Jonathan take the cars outside. With his cars tightly grasped in his hands, Jonathan situated himself in the fort to play. When he played with the cars, the alignment was very important. They must be arranged big to small, right to left. No, they should be arranged end to end with the biggest car in the front of the line, down to the smallest one at the end. Then, the unexpected happened. The first car got too close to the top of the slide and down it went. Hey, this was the best way to race! Before long, Jonathan began carrying the cars outside in a bucket so that it was easier to pick up the finished racers at the bottom of the slide and move them back to the top of the slide for the next race!

By coupling a known setting with new toys and the accidental occurrence of the lead car going down the slide unexpectedly, an engaging play episode ensued. Jonathan's car racing on the slide helped him learn about the relationship of weight to speed, about finding the things you need for play, and about the responsibility of taking care to bring toys back inside. Although real racing is an interest of children who have more sophisticated play patterns, racing the cars down the slide was a very reasonable play progression after the accidental first start. Jonathan began by using the play structure for repetitive physical play. Then the play structure, as a familiar play setting, became part of the known factors in Jonathan's play as a play support. Play choices are child-directed based on experience and discovery. When observing children at play, their play choices are age-related, but they are not age-determined.

assumption NUMBER 4 - *children's play experiences have consequences*

CHILD-DIRECTED PLAY EXPERIENCES, particularly when adults supervise the play but do not interfere, give children the opportunity to experience consequences. A consequence during play is a natural thing. It proves again Newton's third law of motion, the fundamental physical principle that for any action undertaken, there must be an equal reaction. It is critical that children be allowed to engage in play where experience teaches them about positive and negative consequences. In the observation of children, it is evident when the outcome of a play episode is expected and when the product is unexpected. This natural phenomenon of experiencing consequences is one of the best characteristics of child-directed play. It leads children to make predictions about outcomes and helps them revise their previously held assumptions about how things work in their world.

Children never handle information from one domain exclusively at a time. They make assessments across all the domains of learning (physical/sensory, intellectual, ethical and social) while integrating that information to motivate their behavior. Since the only tools we have to judge what is going on in a child's mind is what she says and does, often brief child comments speak volumes to the adult who takes time to listen.

Camping is a family activity, and our family has a many-generation history of recreational camping. As a young family, we would often go camping with my husband's parents. Everyone had jobs to do to prepare for the trip, tasks to do when we arrived and, of course, when we broke camp, still other jobs that had to be done. Our children were always very interested in these special tasks.

One weekend we spent a very enjoyable couple of days in southern Virginia, but now it was time to pack up the RV and head home. It was the "men's job" to tidy the campsite, take the trash to the dumpster and put all of the outside camping gear away. Little red-headed Jimmy followed his Daddy and Pop-Pop around the camper as they carefully rolled up the water hose and put the electric cord back on its reel. Each of the pieces of outside equipment had a place in the storage compartments, and at three years old, Jimmy knew where the equipment went. He raced to the appropriate compartment to open the door and hold it steady as his Dad put each thing away.

Finally, when all of the inside and outside preparations were completed, the best task was saved for last. The trailer had to be hitched to the truck. This is a very careful operation where the truck must be backed up to the trailer so that the ball on the truck hitch is perfectly aligned with the coupling on the trailer.

Jimmy loved the whole process! The ball was covered with grease. A breakaway line was slid into place over the ball. Next, the jack was lowered so that the ball fit into the coupling. An electric line was secured between the truck and the trailer, and, finally, the running lights were checked. What an operation! As the trailer hitch was lowered, Jimmy squatted next to his Dad to observe every detail. On this particular day, when all of my chores were complete, I came out to watch. This small baseball-cap-wearing boy said, "Mommy, us mensis (men) are hooching (hooking) up the trailer, and we're getting geesy (greasy)!"

More than just realizing that jobs needed to be done before we could go home, Jimmy took an active part in the work of his identified group—"the mensis." To his delight, this work had the added benefit of getting greasy! What a great consequence.

assumption NUMBER 5 - children's play experiences are additive

READINESS IS THE VERY POPULAR EDUCATIONAL TERM that means that when children are given information in the correct order and in the proper amount, they are ready to learn. But, children are always learning. They are constantly absorbing information to define aspects of the world as they understand it. Every new piece of information is internally judged to evaluate its purpose and importance against all of the previously assimilated and sorted information. Each nugget that

they receive can be directly helpful, or it can conflict with other information. If an internal conflict of information should arise, the child may display confusion. This is good, because the confusion will cause the child to search for more information to resolve the conflict. With additional attempts to handle new information, the child will move on to successfully handle the new concept with ease.

As the first child in the family, Patty got lots of my undivided attention. On pleasant early spring afternoons, we would walk through the yard, touching the trees and smelling the flowers, and sometimes, we would lie in the grass for an impromptu nap. Patty was just over one year old and everything was fascinating to her. But talking was her highest priority. She would repeat anything and was always willing to comply when someone told her what to say so that people would smile at her. Talking seemed to come naturally to Patty. She started talking at about nine months old with the only two words she mispronounced for a long time—"ushes" for shoes and "ocks" for socks. By the time she was enjoying the adventures in the yard, she already had an active vocabulary of 150 words. She was interested in adding new words to her collection every day. As I walked around the yard with her in my arms, I looked for the things we had named and touched before to see whether she would recall the name and reach out to touch the object again.

One day we were out for a walk, and I reached up to pull a leaf off the maple tree outside our front door. I had given Patty leaves from this tree many times before. But for some reason that I still can't explain to this day, I said, "Look, Patty, green." Her little face spoke of the confusion that must have been charging through her young brain. Yesterday and all the days before, this thing was a leaf—today Mommy said "green." What is green? What is leaf? In an instant, my inner voice told me to show her many things that are green so that she could begin to notice the sameness of the objects and start understanding a second huge language concept—things have names and things also have color. I gave Patty toy cups, dishes and blocks that were all the same shade of green and again said "green." She quickly added the concept of color to her identification of things. This was a huge step for such a young child, yet one that she eagerly took when I gave her the proper input.

For Patty, her mother's first attempt to give her more information was overwhelming. But her determination to learn, adding the new information to her already sorted information, led her to capture a new and powerful concept at an exceptionally early age. Patty had already mastered the concept that things had names and was ready to understand another way to describe the things in her world.

summary

THE FIVE UNDERLYING ASSUMPTIONS ABOUT CHILDREN and play give very direct information about the nature and character of that play.

1. Children are egocentric.

2. Children are compelled to play.

3. Children's play behaviors are age-related, not age-determined.

4. Children's play experiences have consequences.

5. Children's play experiences are additive.

Additionally, these brief statements are helpful in forming a perspective about children's play behaviors.

Children play! Yet, how they play is internally motivated, just like the biological clock that directed their first steps. We hold that in combination with these assumptions, children's play behaviors follow a developmental sequence. That sequence is at the core of the play behavior paradigm and frames the dominant elements of design that should be present in children's play environments. As we begin this journey of looking at play environment design and facilitation, the focus will continue to be on the children and creating environments for play that are laboratories for learning. ❖

the play behavior FRAMEWORK

the play behavior FRAMEWORK

OBSERVING CHILDREN AS THEY PLAY IS ONE OF THE BEST ways to gain an understanding of how holistic human development takes place. The underlying assumptions expressed in the previous chapter are the direct product of our collective research and observation of children across three decades. Now it seems so simple. All children direct their own development by gathering a vast array of information and building the neurological warehouse that will sort, classify and store this huge volume of information that they take in every day. We say "all children" intentionally and with great conviction, for we believe that *all* children who are capable of independent play use the five underlying assumptions in their own time frame to structure and develop their internal systems.

Watching David play is an exciting experience. He really likes to get into cars. Any car in a parking lot that is unlocked will do. But, Mom doesn't think playing in other people's cars is a good idea. So, David enjoys trips to the playground for several reasons. Once in the playground, he wants to try all of the spring riders and likes to repeat the same climbing-sliding pattern many times. He is attracted to everything that moves in the playground but chooses new activities only if Lily, his eight-year-old sister, will get on with him first. David is nine years old and was brain injured at birth.

David learned to walk at five years old, maybe because he wanted to play independently and keep up with Lily. After all, he took his first steps at a playground.

We can't teach children how to think or to move—they must learn how to do that on their own. What we can do is give them an environment rich in the substance that will draw them into engaged play and will lead them to make learning discoveries. Like Grace, the little girl from Iowa, children must be given time within a safe place to play. Two other factors under the direct control of adults influence the productivity of children's play experiences toward developmental advantage. These are the built environments in which children play, like a playground, and the ways that the environment is frequently modified to refresh children's explorations.

During play, children are free to explore two compelling, given characteristics: who they are genetically and what their environment has to offer them. From their play experiences, children blend this information to form their current understanding of how the world works.

Amy Jaffe Barzach, one of the co-founders of the National Center for Boundless Playgrounds, often tells the story of how a chance meeting at a playground changed her life and ultimately the lives of countless children. One afternoon, Amy met a brave little girl in a wheelchair sitting on the sidewalk next to a playground. The girl's disappointed face told the whole story. This was a place where all children want to be included and she was left to sit at the edge, watching the other children play. Her sadness was genuine and simply unforgettable. Like Amy, many of us have similar stories and have seen the bitter disappointment of a child excluded from play—from his peers or siblings.

play behavior FRAMEWORK

BOUNDLESS PLAYGROUNDS PLAY BEHAVIOR FRAMEWORK is child-centered. It is designed to bring attention to the value and purpose of play in the lives of children of all abilities. With a fuller understanding of how children's play behaviors change over the course of their childhood, we are able to focus on the details of how play environments can be designed and facilitated to provide developmental advantage to all children.

The play behavior framework provides child-focused answers to the issues surrounding the design of play environments for children of all abilities. To experience liberty during play, children must be provided an environment free of architectural barriers that limit their range of playful explorations. This is universal design applied to children's play

environments. The other characteristic of a play environment where all children can experience liberty is that the environment must be socially inviting. In child terms, a socially inviting play environment supports children's predictable play behaviors. The focus for all children during play is on "what I can do." Through play, they seek the ways that they can be independent and self-directed in their pursuit of the information they need to forward their own development. The socially inviting play environment is developmentally advantageous for *all* children—children with and without disabilities.

The play behavior framework combines holistic child development philosophy with universal design principles. It is comprised of three guiding concepts—play behavior phases, play environment design criteria and play attraction continuum. Collectively, these concepts share the underlying assumptions and are mutually dependent in their application to the design and facilitation of developmentally advantageous children's play environments that are socially inviting and universally accessible.

play behavior FRAMEWORK

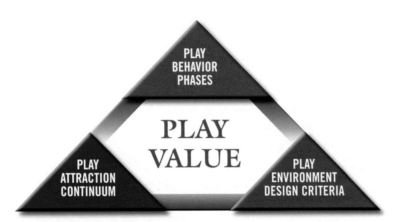

play behavior PHASES

CHILD DEVELOPMENT LITERATURE AND RESEARCH supports the concept of developmental domains that, in turn, take a preeminent role during the course of childhood as the child's preferred information collection system. The principles for play behavior phases couple documented child development research with the observable play behaviors of children. Based on this coupling, the play behaviors are divided into four phases: basic, transitional, complex and interdependent. These four phases cover childhood only—other play phases are likely to follow these into adulthood.

In Chapter 3 of *High Expectations,* we explore the first two play behavior phases, retaining the other two for future publi-

cations on this subject. Here, we explore the characteristics of children in early childhood during engaged play episodes. It is this study and application of the predictable play behaviors of children that should govern the design feature of their play environments. Further, the predictable play behaviors of children give direction of how to constantly refresh the play environment so that they are attracted to developmentally productive engaged play episodes. To achieve consistent engaged play episodes, the characteristics of children's engaged play must be understood so that it can be supported by high-quality design and excellent facilitation.

play environment DESIGN CRITERIA

BASED ON THE PLAY BEHAVIOR PHASES AND WITH consideration of the play attraction continuum, the play environment design criteria include several facets that collectively form a strategy to apply universal design principles to children's play environments. The core facets include distinct play environment groupings for children as they pass through the play behavior phases. Each play environment grouping is rigorous and challenging as well as socially inviting and universally accessible.

The design system of all the play environment groupings is based on children's play behaviors and supports the novelty necessary for engaged play. Within the design system, complexity is a focal element. Children require many opportunities to discover the connections between things and concepts. This is best achieved during play because it is a self-directed and independent activity. Where the play attraction continuum provides novelty to draw children into play, the play environment design criteria are focused on retaining children in engaged play. They provide a sufficiently complex environment to fulfill children's need for a diverse exploration during multiple play episodes. In Chapter 4, the design system that supports the predictable play behaviors of children during early childhood is discussed.

play attraction CONTINUUM

THE OPPORTUNITY TO ENHANCE CHILDREN'S PLAY episodes can be achieved through the play attraction continuum, in which adults provide changes within the play setting and use play facilitation to introduce additional stimuli to children's attention during play. The changes within the play setting and the provision of progressively appropriate materials provide the experience and repetition necessary to gain the full benefit of the developmental substance that children glean during play.

These two characteristics—minor changes to the play environment and the introduction of various materials into play

that are changed regularly—introduce novelty into a play setting. These important characteristics are the subject of Chapter 5. Nov'lication, a term coined by the Boundless Playgrounds Design Team, means variety provided in a play setting that attracts children to engaged play. It is key to a great, child-focused play environment in which adults are committed to delivering maximum play benefit.

Naomi is a beautiful little girl with a charming smile, a quick wit and bouncy blond curls. One day I had the pleasure to meet Naomi and her mother at the early intervention center where she had been enrolled since she was a baby.

At four years old, Naomi was confident and always at the center of the activities in the building. The playground had been the place where Naomi and her friends that used wheelchairs were limited in their play explorations. Betsy Farmer, the center founder and director, could see that the playground needed to match the terrific environment the center had created for its children inside. And with that commitment, she launched her crusade to build a playground where all of the children could play together.

This was my first visit to the center since the new Boundless Playground had opened six months earlier. I was excited to see the children playing. Betsy's greeting was followed by an introduction to

Naomi's mother, Jackie, who asked me to follow her to the playground to meet Naomi. Of course I wanted to meet her—but I was not prepared for the greeting I received from Naomi that morning. As we walked out the door, Jackie called, "Naomi, this is Miss Jean. She designed your playground."

"Miss Jean! I've been waiting for you! I have to show you all the things I can do on my playground!"

With that, she turned in her wheelchair and zoomed off, making sure that I was following her. She played in the water at the play table and talked into the talk tube. She used the transfer to crawl in the tunnel and go down the slide. She was everywhere! I was overwhelmed with emotion. Each time she turned to be sure that I was still following and watching her, I had to discreetly brush the tears of joy from my face. (I don't think she would have understood that those tears expressed great happiness to be watching "all the things that she could do!")

Six months earlier she had been on the sidelines—now she was in the center of things, heading the follow-the-leader game! She had learned to climb on this playground and later would walk down the aisle to accept her kindergarten graduation diploma.

summary

SOMETIMES WE SHOULD STOP AND ASK, "Why do we give children places and time to play?" If the answer to that question incorporates the five underlying assumptions that children need to play because it is the best way for them to build their internal systems, then it stands to reason that the only rational way to build play environments is in harmony with the predictable manners that children play so that they can find what they need to advance their own development. That harmony is found in the Boundless Playgrounds play behavior framework. Playgrounds that are designed to provide experiences according to children's predictable play behaviors can have a profound impact on the lives of all children! ❧

the predictable play BEHAVIORS OF CHILDREN

the predictable play BEHAVIORS OF CHILDREN

T O SAY THAT CHILDREN'S PLAY BEHAVIORS ARE PREDICTABLE is stating the obvious. Each of us has engaged in the baby games of dropping the spoon over the side of the high chair, peek-a-boo, and countless other activities with young children. We aren't thinking about what the children are learning as we play. Maybe we should.

She didn't notice the pretty colors on the ground or hear the sound of laughter from her friends in the sandbox. Teresa, who has Down syndrome, was focused on each step in her balancing loop. She had been reluctant to step across open spaces, so the first time she moved from the balance beam to the round pod was a great triumph. (Many children with Down syndrome are challenged by the motor planning required by balancing activities and therefore avoid developing these sophisticated movement skills.) But no one was watching. It was a personal victory! So around and around she moved— across the balance beam to the pods. One, two, three, four, five, six! Jump off into an Olympic victory stance and then start the balance circuit again. Right foot, left foot, sometimes pausing on two feet, around and around the balancing loop, testing how to place her feet, where to

keep her arms, trying not to fall! With each completed loop, the victory stance. Teresa's determined face told the story of her sweet success!

In some ways, it has been the greatest blessing to design playgrounds for children with and without disabilities, and then watch them use the play environment to explore their emerging skills. Their personal determination to master the world has accentuated the steps in the development process so distinctly that now, after years of observation, the steps are easily recognizable in all children, regardless of ability or disability. Like Teresa, all children begin to master sensory information and movement skills through the repetition provided during independent self-directed play.

These repetitions are interesting because to a casual observer, the children appear to be doing *exactly* the same thing over and over again. But upon closer examination, each loop has many variables. We have termed these repetitive activities loops because this child-directed action is a continuous circuit of activity.

Additionally, when others (either adults or children) insert themselves to interrupt the loop, developmental consequences can be great. Looping is the first observable play behavior children use to build their understanding of how the world works.

play behavior PHASES

MANY AUTHORS AND RESEARCHERS HAVE CATALOGED various ways to speak about the observations of children during the course of their development. Toward Developmental Advantage: A Supporting Text for High Expectations is the companion CD-ROM that accompanies this book. It examines the literature on these subjects and provides further validation.

To more fully understand the aspects of our defined children's play behaviors, we have identified several key factors that can be tracked across childhood to help determine where the children are developmentally.

The key factors of play behavior phases are:

Key Factor 1—Domain

Key Factor 2—Observable Play Behavior

Key Factor 3—Play Type

Key Factor 4—Acting-Out Behavior

The characteristics of each of these key factors will become evident as we move through this discussion, so we won't belabor the point here.

Before we proceed with our discussion and analysis of the first play behavior phase, however, it seems reasonable to state our focus on the nature of engaged play. Play is important in the lives of children because it allows them to direct their choices and experience consequences, thereby making related discoveries and enjoying the developmental benefits of being self-directed. For engaged play to occur children must be at the core of the activity; they must be a/the primary initiator of the play event where they direct the outcome. The separation from adult interaction, taken by children to the level of engaged play, allows them to make choices that give them the autonomy to experience consequences, master a new movement skill or make a new discovery.

basic play PHASE

THE YOUNG CHILD'S DETERMINATION TO ACHIEVE independence is manifested in his diligence to learn to move and his persistence in gathering sensory information. The time span between an infant in his crib and that child walking around the furniture as a toddler is brief, yet it is one that is full of information gathering. Piaget and others have stated that the first preferred domain for gathering and organizing information is the physical/sensory domain. In watching children during this least sophisticated developmental period, most of their efforts seem to center on touching, tasting, seeing, hearing, smelling and moving. When given the opportunity to be self-directed, they choose to go on fact-finding missions.

Like most children in the basic play phase, José seems to be a very determined 2½-year-old fellow.

On the day that I observed him at an Easter Seals Center, he was busy playing by himself in a motor skill looping pattern. Climbing up the ship's ladder to the connecting platform, he arranged himself at the top of the slide. Once he was set, down the slide he went. Upon landing at the bottom of the slide, it was back to the ship's ladder to climb up again. During this free-play episode, he made this circuit countless times, only being distracted by his peers who were using the same loop or by a caregiver who suggested that he should move on and try something else.

It is important to note that José was grasping the handrail with only his right hand. His left side had been damaged early in his life, and he preferred to use his right arm exclusively for strength and balance. (In the photo, notice that his right foot is placed on the second step — he was trying a new way to get up the steps. Soon he discovered that this was not going to be a successful way up.) During repetitive loops, José always led with his strong side—the right. (Other children playing in loops will change to lead with both hands and both feet, trying as many combinations as occur to them.) All children learn the best ways to move by testing out their theories during independent self-directed play.

When José reached the platform, he used his right hand for balance as he transitioned to the seated position at the top of the slide. The combinations of movements to achieve the sitting position varied each time he reached the top of the slide.

Sometimes he sat down on the platform on the inside of the slide hood, and then slipped through the slide hood to the top of the slide. Other times, he used the handholds in the slide hood to aid in his balance as he sat or used the slide rail for balance. Sometimes, his right leg was bent first, other times, his left.

His focus on this motor skill loop—the activity of climbing the ship's ladder, sitting down, then using the slide—was consuming. The other people within his vicinity were of little interest. Interacting with them seemed to be nothing more than a distraction. José managed to maneuver around the teacher at the bottom of the ship's ladder with just a slight nudge on his part to begin another loop.

let's take a closer look

José was clearly in the midst of an engaged play episode.

His independent play activities show us many of the important aspects of children during the basic play phase. As we analyze José's play behavior, the key factors of the play behavior phases will appear, as will what constitutes an engaged play episode for children in the basic play phase. In addition, the beneficial characteristics of the play environment that aid in the basic play phase child's discoveries will be revealed.

Key Factor 1—Domain

José is primarily interested in collecting information within the physical/sensory domain. He is internally directing his play choices so that he can gather both the sensory experiences that are part of climbing and sliding and perfecting his movement skills at the same time. During each repetition, José tries something a little different-how he places his hands and feet, the order of his movements, even when and where he sits down to use the slide. He likes to touch many things during his circuit and sometimes bangs on things to listen to the sounds they make in response to his action.

José must internally couple his movements with the sensory experiences that are a consequence of his movements. This is called sensory integration. These couplings are the foundation of José's understanding of cause and effect and also build the neurological pathways that will help him master a variety of sensory inputs and more and more advanced movement skills. His motor planning already is a reflection of many sophisticated movement skills. Sometimes he uses a cross-lateral pattern (first step, right foot up; second step, left foot to the next step; third step, right foot to

the next step; fourth step, left foot to the next step, etc.) in his climbing in place of the less sophisticated marking-time pattern (first step, right foot up, then the left foot to the same step; second step, right foot up, then the left foot to the same step, etc.). He has developed a successful system for mastering new skills because he is willing to try many ways to do something, capitalizing on the learning that happens during repetition. This is the mark of a child who will continue to forward his own development through experience.

Key Factor 2—Observable Play Behavior

Looping is the observable play behavior of children in this first play phase. It is characterized by intense repetitions that have a simple similarity. Each repetition of the activity is not an exact duplication—it is duplication with variety. A loop harvests successful movement combinations and points out what movement combinations are unsuccessful. During a loop, children will vary their path to include the gathering of new sensory information or to avoid an interruption from another child or an adult.

The most telling characteristic of a looping play pattern is that it is a self-determined action. This is not an activity that looks like follow the leader. The child by her own free will engages in play that displays a repeated pattern and is highly focused on achieving many repetitions without interruption. These loops in an outdoor play environment often are like the one José was engaged in during his self-directed play episode or like the little girl on the balancing circuit at the beginning of the chapter. We have also observed children playing in a loop by filling a bucket, carrying it to a sand wheel, dumping it, going back to the same spot in the sand box, filling the bucket, etc.

The three classifications of looping play behavior are:

1. **Seek and Find:** like dropping an object from the high chair repetitions

2. **Sensory Gathering:** like the multi-sensory repetitive explorations children do to investigate new objects or surroundings

3. **Motor Skill:** like movement repetitions on a play structure

A loop is not finished until the child is satisfied. She will complete an unpredictable number of repetitions with an equally unpredictable number of variations, and then she will be finished. At that point she will walk away and engage in another play activity that may also display the same looping

pattern. Engaged play for children in the basic play phase always seems to have this repetitive characteristic.

Key Factor 3—Play Type

José was happy to be by himself during his play episode on the playground. During the basic play phase, most children are very content to explore by themselves. They often see other children as an obstacle or a barrier to be contended with during their independent investigations. We classify this play type as autonomous. In this phase, children are most likely to become fully engaged in play if they are allowed to play alone.

At times, children in the basic play phase watch each other, but they don't often converse to enhance their play experiences or share resources. The best way to provide for a conflict-free play environment for the children in this play phase is to always supply multiple play elements. Children seem to learn to share best in an atmosphere of abundance as opposed to an atmosphere of scarcity.

Key Factor 4—Acting-Out Behavior

Given the previously stated preferred domain and the other characteristics of children in this play phase, it should not come as a surprise that their most likely acting–out behavior is with their body. What prompts a child in the basic play phase to act out? Most often children act out when their loops are interrupted! (Otherwise, they go along with most adult directions fairly well.) When children are interrupted during an engaged play episode, they use their bodies in any way they can to continue their loop. If an adult is the source of the interruption, children will scream, wiggle, and otherwise try to get away so that they can continue their loop. Their reactions are similar when another child is the cause of the interruption, but pushing and biting might also be included in their repertoire.

If a child has developed language as a tool for getting her way, she will try to negotiate "One more time." Based on previous experiences when an adult offered another five minutes or one more time, the child will also attempt this strategy to prolong her loop. Continuing the loop pattern until they have been satisfied is a primary objective for children in the basic play phase.

basic play behavior PHASE REVIEW

The key factors of this phase are

Domain	Sensory/motor
Observable Play Behavior	Looping
Play Type	Autonomous
Acting-Out Behavior	With the body

transitional play PHASE

AS CHILDREN BEGIN THE SHIFT IN PREFERENCE TO THE second play behavior phase, they don't suddenly abandon their usage of the basic play behaviors. In fact, the change is gradual. The new play behavior is adopted and begins to take preeminence as the old play behaviors are used less frequently. As we mentioned in the underlying assumptions, this next play behavior phase is built on the skills and learning that occurred in the previous play behavior phase. Hence, we say children's play experiences are additive.

During the transitional play behavior phase, children combine the physical/sensory domain of the basic behavior phase with the intellectual domain of the transitional play phase to explore play in a whole new way. They add "stuff" to the equation to learn about a wide variety of concepts. All of their interest in developing their ability to move is still progressing, yet not as a sole focus. They also continue to display interest in having sensory experiences, but all things are not explored as often with the mouth. Touching, smelling and seeing are now the more common ways to discover the unknown.

Grace, the 4-year-old little girl we met in the first chapter, is interested in including "stuff" into her play episodes. Stuff is a Boundless Playgrounds technical term for toys or natural materials that a child finds within a play environment and selects to include in her play. Stuff can be grass, pine needles, nuts, leaves, moss, stones, pinecones, berries or sticks, things that children appropriate for their engaged play episode. Any of these materials can be specially assigned a role during play or they can be used for experiments of the child's design.

During a trip to the local playground, Grace made an amazing discovery—small nuts were scattered around the ground! "How many nuts are there? They are all different but about the same size. These will be fun to play with." Soon, Grace was busy gathering these nuts and carrying them in her turned-up shirt pouch.

Somehow, these nuts were an important part of her play that day. After she had collected enough, the nuts were carried onto the play platform for sorting and organizing. "Maybe these little nuts should be a collection to take home to show Mommy."

On the play platform, all of the nuts are emptied from the pouch. "They feel smooth and they are so round. I think they can roll down the slide. Listen to the sounds they make as they bounce all the way down. When you send a lot of them at once, they make more noise than when you only send one down at a time. I'll send a lot!

"Some of them slid off the end of the slide! How will I find them again? I wonder… when they go faster, do they go further off the end of the slide? I better slide down myself to gather them up again so I can find out what happens.

"Those other children are looking at my little nuts; maybe they want to play, too! They can help me pick up the nuts to run them down the slide again! Hey, don't put my nuts in your pockets— they're mine! Give them back to me! You hurt my feelings!"

let's take a closer look

Grace has discovered the pathway to an engaged play episode-opportunistic branching. Her determination to pursue independent play activities shows us many of the important aspects of children during transitional play phase. As we analyze Grace's play behavior, the key factors of the play behavior phases will appear, as will what constitutes an engaged play episode for children in the transitional play phase. In addition, the beneficial characteristics of the play environment that aid in the transitional play phase child's discoveries will be revealed.

Key Factor 1—Domain

What Grace finds exciting during her visit to the playground is the very next thing she needs most to forward her own development. Now, she prefers to collect information associated with the development of the intellectual domain. Grace is interested in determining the ways that things compare to each other and how things are related. She experiments with many things to see what happens. Her investigation sometimes looks very messy and the broader her field of inquiry, the greater her understanding of how the physical world works. This is how she is developing her intellect. Her learning is what makes play so interesting. This type of manipulative play combines movement and sensory experiences with the curiosity of a young scientist.

Questions are plentiful, but nothing seems to satisfy the inquiring mind like the hands-on, first-person, let-me-do-it-myself, self-directed play of children during this play phase.

The nuts provided Grace with an excellent combination of

characteristics for use during her play episode. The nuts were plentiful and easy to transport and had a sufficient number of variables and similarities to make them interesting. Note that Grace's engaged play episode with the little nuts was opportunistic. She used them in her play because she just happened to find them. Based on previous play experiences, Grace spontaneously yet in a somewhat evolutionary manner determined how she would use the nuts during her play. This opportunistic characteristic is indicative of early branching behavior play in which children choose any interesting materials for play that they just happen to discover. Hence the earliest manifestation of this play behavior is demonstrated by the child's opportunistic choices of materials for an engaged play episode. We have defined branching as a more sophisticated play behavior that couples movement and sensory experiences with the child-initiated gathering of loose parts to expand play in play episodes under the child's direction.

As children continue to use branching play behaviors, they will seek out materials that fulfill an aspect of a play episode. This is called selective branching. A good example of this "resourcing" of materials is when children search for a large leaf to serve as a plate or figure out how to get some water into the sandbox so that they can mold the sand better. This is a tangible demonstration of child problem-solving during play—proof that play is real development in action.

So why not just take toys to the playground? Children seem to benefit the most from play episodes where some things are known, like the playground structure, and some things are newly discovered. As soon as Grace found the nuts, she launched an experiment. Interestingly, she had not decided to roll the nuts down the slide at first. She had simply sat down to unload the nuts and play with them by inspecting and sorting them. The complexity of her play episode grew as she followed her interest and imagination.

A further characteristic of children's play during this transitional play phase revolves around the manner in which they acquire and use language. Children talk to themselves during engaged play. This is really thinking out loud. The words are an expression of their discoveries, their observations, and their plans. In the transitional play phase, children think out loud to confirm to themselves the truth of their findings

during play. The words travel out of their own mouths back into their own ears. This dual reinforcement of facts helps children establish the neurological connections between related bits of information they have stored in their brain. This pattern is repeated hundreds of times a day to form the framework of knowledge and intellect. All of this happens because children go to a playground (an area they are familiar with), can find things like nuts (new discoveries), and are given the opportunity to play with them in an independent, self-directed way. Great work for a child!

Key Factor 2—Observable Play Behavior

Children in the transitional play phase are compelled to gather, arrange, sort, and compare to determine the relationships between objects, just like Grace did with her nuts. It is the characteristic of adding things to vary play that provides children with new information needed for relational insights and expanded development. These expanded but repetitive experiences are part of branching. The child is situated in a place for play, "needs" something additional to sustain play, branches out to get it, and continues in engaged play.

When allowed to independently select activities, children in the transitional play phase often gather natural and loose-part materials to integrate sensory and movement experiences. While they play, they also observe other children playing. By copying what they see other children doing at play, they expand their own repertoire of play experiences.

There are three classifications of branching play behavior:

1. **Opportunistic**: child plays with "stuff" they just happen to find when engaged in play

2. **Observational**: child mirrors or copies the play activities of another child or mimics the behaviors of an adult through role-playing

3. **Selective**: child seeks out "stuff" to support a specific aspect of an imaginary play episode

Grace's branching is a more sophisticated play behavior than the looping play behavior displayed by José because it couples movement and sensory experiences with loose parts into play episodes under the child's direction. The primary difference between looping and branching play behaviors is the ongoing addition of loose parts or natural materials to provide variation to each play episode. Consider these other example of branching:

- A child uses a bucket to scoop sand, dumps it in a pile, finds a spoon in the sand, returns to the bucket, spoons the sand into the bucket, dumps it in a pile, repeats – this is an example of opportunistic branching.

- A child sees another child playing with a bucket and filling a hole with water in the sandbox, takes his bucket to the spigot to get water, takes the bucket to the place where a hole is dug in the sand, dumps the water into the hole in the sand, watches the water disappear, repeats – this is an example of observational branching.

- A child is perched at the top of the slide. He rolls a die cast car down the slide, slides down, retrieves the first car, goes to a loose-parts area to get a second car, returns to the top of the slide, races the two cars down the slide, repeats – this is an example of selective branching.

As children branch during a play episode, they continue using autonomous play experiences coupled with parallel play to collect observations. They also are building understanding of the way the world works and how they can control or manipulate it. Additionally, the play preferences of children in the transitional play phase include their interest in finding and using small places to play. Early childhood educators have long identified the need for the inclusion of cozy spots, or semiprivate spaces, in the design of interior space. Preschool classrooms often feature several small nooks where one or two children can gather for a play episode. This need for designated small spaces in the outdoor play environment is even greater, since the scope of the outdoors is larger than within a building setting. The cozy spot is a preferred

location for basing a play episode and launching from that spot to gather the natural materials and loose parts.

Key Factor 3—Play Type

Play has evolved for children like Grace. Now she is interested in play in parallel with other children. This means that children can each have a successful play episode doing the same activities, each with their own things. If Grace has a thing to play with and a second child has a similar object to play with and they both have enough space to play, life is good. If Grace has something to play with and the other child wants it, the result is a conflict. Or, if the second child crowds into Grace's space, that might also result in conflict.

A good example of Grace playing in parallel would be when Mary, who is also collecting nuts, joins Grace. The two girls carry the nuts to the slide and roll them down. Each child has her own collection of nuts. Each of them is using the slide and collecting her own nuts at the bottom of the slide. They might even meet at the top of the slide and roll their nuts down the slide together. This scenario would produce a successful play episode for each child.

Grace is happy to include Mary in her play episode as long as she acts in the ways that Grace predicts. In this case, Grace has found the little nuts at the park. She could get many more, but these nuts have become her possessions. She insists on maintaining control over her things. Grace has learned by experience that to have some control over your possessions, you must assert your ownership.

When Mary was first attracted to the slide by the sound of the nuts, Grace was willing to include her in the play. Very soon she realized that Mary was not going to participate as she directed. This was in conflict with Grace's independent direction for the play episode. This is known as a play conflict, clearly one that can be predicted by supervising adults. Grace is engaged in her branching play behavior. If Mary begins to take Grace's appropriated play materials, a conflict in play may happen. Reminding Mary where to find more nuts on the ground could prevent a conflict.

Key Factor 4—Acting-Out Behavior

If Grace reaches a point where she feels she has lost control of her play property, she will act out by using her toys as weapons. In this play phase, children see their toys and the stuff they play with as tools, as extensions of themselves. They will throw the nuts, or use a stick or a block as an implement to hit someone else with when they are provoked. Adult supervision within a play environment should foresee this frustration and intervene to prevent an injury to either child.

transitional play behavior PHASE REVIEW

The key factors of this phase are

Domain	Intellectual
Observable Play Behavior	Branching
Play Type	Parallel
Acting-Out Behavior	Using toys as weapons

summary

THE BASIC AND TRANSITIONAL PLAY PHASES ARE THE FIRST two of the four childhood play phases, those that are reflective of the play behaviors of many preschool children. Future texts will elaborate the play characteristics of children as they become more sophisticated in their play behaviors throughout childhood in the complex and interdependent play phases.

Children of all abilities who are capable of independent play display predictable play behaviors. Therefore, the play environments in which they play should provide an abundance of opportunities for the children to explore their world. Engaged play gives children the developmental substance to build their neurological framework and intellect, advance their movement skills, and become proficient at integrating sensory information. Play is the child's greatest strategy to prepare them for life.

Play environments are an interesting dichotomy—one part simplicity and one part laboratory! As we continue to unwrap this amazing thing we call a play environment, we will look at how an outdoor space can support the needs of all children, with and without disabilities, during play. ❧

first two play BEHAVIOR PHASES

Key Factors	Basic	Transitional
Domain	Physical/Sensory	Intellectual
Observable Play Behavior	Looping	Branching
Play Type	Autonomous	Parallel
Acting-Out Behavior	With the body	Using toys as weapons

pattern SUPPORTS

pattern SUPPORTS

NOW THAT WE KNOW WHOM THE PLAYERS ARE AND HOW they can be expected to perform, we must begin to set the stage!

For repetitive play episodes to be of a fully engaged, compelling nature and of developmental benefit to children, an environment where independent, self-directed play is encouraged must be provided. Open-ended play, with multiple choices and no wrong way to play (unless it hurts someone), is at the core of engaged play. Great care in the design and facilitation of the play setting is required to achieve a child-focused environment with these characteristics.

She had come to visit for a couple of days with Mommy and Daddy. Several bags of things had been packed for the trip so that Autumn, three years old, would have plenty to do while they made the rounds to various family homes. She clearly knew where her favorites were and there was no stopping her from diving right in to the bags to get what she wanted.

First came the floor length "dancing girl" skirt, then the shoes, tiara, glasses and finally, a feather boa. Was she gorgeous! Appropriate comments were made about her beauty, and then came the performance. Autumn twirled and spun, the feathers of the boa floating to the floor in rhythm with her movements. For a while she watched for the reactions of her adoring audience. And then it happened. She heard her own music and her conversation became exclusively self-focused. She was still playing in my living room where I could enjoy the sound of her voice in song and delight in the artistry of her movements, but she had gone to that magical place of engaged play. She was completely absorbed. What a treat to watch it happen!

The play behavior framework outlined in Chapter 2 tells us that as we understand the play behaviors of children, we should follow that evidence in the design of play environments. In addition to that play behavior framework, eight general design principles will have a beneficial affect on the play-usefulness of the play environment for all children, with and without disabilities, when applied to the design of play environments.

The eight design principles of a fully integrated play environment for *all* children in the basic and transitional play phases are the following:

1. Absence of architectural barriers—a barrier-free environment
2. Developmentally distinct play areas supporting the predictable play behaviors of children
3. Diversity of movement sensations and experiences
4. Many loose manipulative parts and natural materials in

the playground for children to use during each engaged play episode

5. Opportunities to play autonomously and alongside peers

6. Inclusion of semi-enclosed spots

7. Provision for being up high and viewing the world from an elevated vista

8. Rigorous and challenging places to play

… So that all children can play, each at their highest level of ability.

a new way to design PLAY ENVIRONMENTS

THE IMPLICATIONS FOR AND APPLICATION OF SOME OF these design principles may be obvious. But the second principle on the list, developmentally distinct play spaces reflective of the characteristics of children's play behaviors as they progress through various developmental play phases, is a new way of designing children's play environments. Heretofore, public play environments have been designed based on children's ages with a separate area for children 2 to 5 years old and another separate play space for children 5 to 12 years old. It is important to clearly indicate with signage in public playgrounds the group of children for whom the environment is designed. Since the most conventional method to convey this information is based on the age of

children, this system should persist. (In Chapter 7 of *High Expectations* this issue is addressed further.) The other relevant issue with regard to the design of children's play environments is carrying capacity, that is, the number of children that can be expected to achieve engaged play within a play setting. These two issues are factors of consideration in play environment development due to their importance on the quality of a child's play experience.

Play areas for *all* children should provide a distinct, interesting, developmentally advantageous, rigorous and challenging place to play, a place where engaged play happens. These play areas are called play environment groupings (PEGs) and are divided into four categories, ALPHA, BETA, GAMMA, AND DELTA. The ALPHA PEG suits the development needs for children in the basic and transitional play phases. The BETA PEG addresses the needs of children within the transitional and complex phases of play. The GAMMA PEG

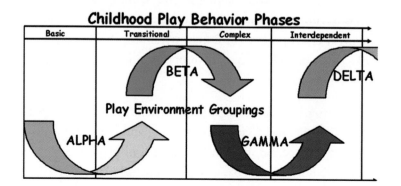

meets the needs of the children playing in the complex and interdependent play phases. The DELTA PEG addresses the play interests for young people in the interdependent play phase and beyond.

With the exception of very early childhood, children are always in the midst of two preferred play behaviors. Therefore, it is reasonable to design play settings to support this developmental reality.

The design system that supports independent, self-directed, repetitive play for children who are in the basic and transitional play phases are called pattern supports. The purpose of establishing a design system is to offer direction about the elements of play and the configuration of components within a play environment to enhance the play experiences of children. Pattern supports, the design system for the ALPHA PEG, must provide a diversity of opportunities for looping and branching play behaviors.

The extent of the developmental benefit provided by repetitive series of play activities, like looping and branching, is not fully understood. But, under all types of play circumstances, children in the basic and transitional play phases choose to play in repetitive series. These series, in all of their manifestations, are the basis for the design system that is expressed for an ALPHA play environment grouping.

A combination of characteristics must be present to create developmental advantage for children in a play environment. The play components that are selected must match the child's ability and provide suitable challenge along the developmental continuum. In other words, play components should be selected that require progressively sophisticated motor planning skill. It is the combination of correctly selected play components configured in compliance with children's predictable play behaviors that leads to developmental advantage.

In addition to playing in loops or branching, children must find interesting places to play to become fully engaged. Children look for places to play that support their interests, like child-sized spots that are cozy, or places that have interesting sensory discoveries, like light and shadows or interesting things to touch or hear. Children may use these spots as part of a loop, or they could use the cozy spot as a base for their branching play experience. They are also attracted to loose parts and natural materials within the play environment.

designing for looping PLAY BEHAVIOR

L OOPING DURING PLAY GIVES CHILDREN MULTIPLE, repetitive opportunities to collect information from the senses and from movement. On a play structure, looping could include *going up a climber to a platform, sitting at the top of the slide, sliding down the slide, repeat.* This diagram shows several circuits that support children playing in loops.

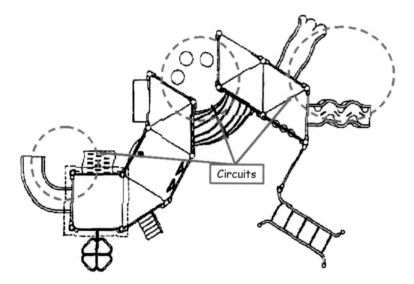

Circuits

Another typically repetitive sensory gathering loop used by children includes *touching, smelling and looking at an unfamiliar plant like a lambs ear leaf – it is fuzzy to the touch, something unexpected by most children.* Children also collect sensory information by many different types of movement like bouncing, rocking and spinning. During engaged play children will use play equipment that supplies the interesting information about vestibular movement to add to their understanding about sensory integration.

Repetition provides the opportunity to compare the information from one loop to the next. Children sort these experiences, compare and contrast them and store them for future use. The ability to see the beginning of the circuit, even as the end is reached, serves to stabilize the loop in the play *pattern* of the child and *supports* the need for repetition in play to build functional neurological pathways. When included in a composite play structure, pattern supports address the need for a full array of sensory and movement experiences designed to support the predictable looping and branching play behaviors of children.

Pattern supports for motor skill looping on a structure are those in which a series of play component parts are in immediate proximity. This is called a circuit. The child uses the play components within the circuit while displaying looping behavior. There are three distinct types of motor skill loops possible in an ALPHA PEG that should be supported by circuits, (1) climber/slide (2) balancing and (3) change in posture. The carrying capacity of each circuit is five children (one child on the climber, one on the platform, one on the slide, two in transit). If an ALPHA PEG is proposed to support 10 children during a play session, the configuration should have at least two circuits that will support the children making motor skill loops.

Indirect circuits on a structure are those that are discovered during play. Facilitation of an expanded looping pattern is the product of a child linking several distant and maybe disconnected play components together in a repetitive route of travel. Children choose to pass more immediate or proximal components that can be used for access in a repetitive looping pattern in preference for components that are more distant but usable in the expanded repetitive looping pattern. Children who have become more sophisticated in their play will extend their loops to gather more information. For indirect circuits to add carrying capacity to the play environment there must be a surplus of climbers in the climber to slide ratio.

One of the best ways to provide a developmentally advantageous play environment for children in the basic play phase is with as broad a spectrum of sensory and movement experiences as possible. A variety of play components should be used to construct each pattern support. Select a different climber and slide for each of the circuits. Select slides that give different sensory experiences—slides with bumps, right

turns or with rollers so that children can feel the slide in many positions. The climbers should be selected so that many different motor patterns can be tested and perfected through multiple play episodes. Climbers that provide children opportunities to use one foot at a time climbing or a cross-lateral movement can be effective in helping them master the various ways to move their bodies. There should be a minimum climber to slide ratio of one climber for each slide. More climbers than slides are preferable as this design characteristic adds carrying capacity to the play environment. If this play environment will be used in combination with other play spaces, select different components than are available in the other play environment(s).

Children in the basic play phase are predictably going to play autonomously, or, as they move toward the next, more sophisticated play behavior, in parallel with other children. To minimize the likelihood of altercations among children during their engaged play episodes, it is recommended that the play environment provide an abundance of play activities. This will enrich the play environment for the children while reducing conflicts during play. Scarcity of play materials and limited play experiences can lead to frustrated children who resort to their predictable acting-out behaviors to gather the information they are compelled to obtain during play.

The following three guidelines provide an abundance of play activities in a play setting. A play setting should have

1. A variety of play experiences

2. A large selection of similar things with variations on a theme

3. Multiples of the same things

If the goal is to provide a truly enriched play environment, select a healthy measure of guidelines 1 and 2 with limited application of guideline 3, since it is the least effective method to add to the dynamic of children's play. Guidelines 2 and 3 will be discussed further in Chapter 5.

Cozy spots are also required as a pattern support, and an ALPHA PEG presents many desirable characteristics for cozy spots. One key consideration is making all the cozy spots different. In addition, so that most of these appealing play locations (70 percent or more) are usable by children with mobility impairments, they should be on an elevated composite play structure with ramp access or at ground level and surrounded by unitary rubber surfacing. (This type of surfacing requires very little routine maintenance, and even in conditions where routine maintenance is

marginal, this surface continues to provide a barrier-free safety surface within the use zone of play equipment.) At least one side of the cozy spot should have a minimum clear opening of 36 inches wide and 48 inches of head clearance. Cozy spots with less than 48 inches of headroom will be useful to children during play but will not facilitate full inclusion during play. Consider providing one cozy spot for every five children who will be using the play environment. A cozy spot can be under an elevated play platform, a nook created with bushes, a tunnel at ground level or between platforms or a small roofed structure.

Maximum developmental advantage for *all* children can be provided within an ALPHA PEG with a ramped composite play structure. This provision in a play environment allows all children regardless of ability the opportunity to experience height. Being up high and viewing the world from a greater vista helps children develop their perspective. With the chance to see all sides of their play environment from one spot, children formulate a fuller understanding of space and the relationships of the places they are familiar with. This is a fundamental building block for many physical and spatial understandings. In some play environments, the provision of experiencing height can be accomplished by means of natural elements like hills with accessible pathways. Combine the natural height with interesting things to do (like a periscope) and interesting places to be (like a small fort) to add complexity.

Since sensory experiences are compelling for all children in the basic play phase, play events that make sounds or panels with elements to move that have a variety of colors are interesting. Play equipment structures that bounce, rock or spin are appealing. These play features should be selected to provide both autonomous and parallel play opportunities and be installed in the play environment over accessible surfacing so that all children can gain the developmental advantage that these play features provide. Children will also gravitate to cozy spots that have cubbies or shelves for them to place the things they gather and sort.

Another way to provide a diverse sensory and movement experience is with a tricycle path. (Notice the humps and bumps in this tricycle pathway!) This play feature must be part of the original playground environment design so that it is allotted an appropriate amount of space and doesn't encroach on the use zones of other play features. The selection of the surfacing materials for the tricycle path will govern some of its design choices, but the best pathways have intersecting loops with interesting sensory experiences built in. A tricycle pathway can serve as the accessible circulation path system throughout the play environment. Many exciting play experiences can revolve around a well-designed tricycle pathway. Therefore, more specific design information is provided about tricycle paths in Chapter 7.

pattern supports for looping
PLAY BEHAVIOR

1. Objects to touch, move, smell, see and hear

2. Small, child-sized places with sensory discoveries

3. Slides that afford variation in sensory experience like slight turns, bumps, rollers or waves

4. Climbers that provide children opportunities to use one foot at a time or a cross-lateral movement while climbing

5. Abundance within the play environments by providing a variety of natural materials and multiple loose parts

6. Platforms that are different shapes and heights, with and without roofs

7. Tunnels that are straight or partial curves with peeping holes

8. Movement play features like spring rockers, spring-centered see-saws and whirls

9. Balancing activities like a straight or curved beam or stepping forms

10. Bridges that are solid, that move, or are made of pipe

11. A pathway for tricycles that provides opportunities for choice and discovery

Each of the variations, and the combination of these variations, afford children the liberty to explore the environment. They discover a range of sensory experiences and how to independently move their bodies within the play environment. This leads to a greater sense of independence and self-worth.

designing for branching PLAY BEHAVIOR

As NOTED IN CHAPTER 3, AS CHILDREN BECOME MORE sophisticated in their play behaviors they are compelled to gather, arrange, sort, and compare to determine the relationships between objects. It is the characteristic of adding things to vary play that provides children with new information needed for relational insights and expanded development. These expanded but repetitive experiences provide the basis for the term branching and are part of the transitional play phase. Branching is a more sophisticated play behavior because it couples movement and sensory experiences with loose parts into play episodes under the child's direction.

Examples of branching cited in Chapter 3 include the following:

- A child uses a bucket to scoop sand, dumps it in a pile, goes to get a spoon, returns to the bucket, spoons the sand into the bucket, dumps it in a pile, repeats.

- A child is perched at the top of the slide. He rolls a die cast car down the slide, slides down, retrieves the first car, goes to a loose-parts area to get a second car, returns to the top of the slide, races the two cars down the slide, repeats.

- A child pours water in a bucket, takes the bucket to the place where a hole is dug in the sand, dumps the water into the hole in the sand, determines how long the water stays in the hole, repeats.

Opportunistic branching in a play environment is demonstrated by those patterns in which natural materials or loose parts are found in the immediate vicinity of the playing child. The materials or parts are brought into the child's play to extend the engaged play experience. Sometimes he will traverse a longer distance to select natural materials or to acquire loose parts to bring them into his play pattern. If, during the distance traveled, the child continues to focus on his play and is not distracted from his play, then that child is using a selective branching play pattern. So, it could be said that children begin opportunistically gathering stuff to add to their play and as their sophistication in play increases they become selective about adding materials to their engaged play episodes.

> They were very busy at the park. The project in the sand was going very well as long as they kept the sand wet. The dry sand crumbled as fast as the boys could build it. Wet sand works best. "Let's get some water from the fountain to keep it wet! Hey, Jessie, you get the water while we keep working."

Children at play in the transitional phase also observe other children playing. They copy these observations to expand their own repertoire of play experience. This is considered parallel play and is an example of observational branching.

ALPHA PEGs should provide multiple, manipulative play experience choices for the play purpose of branching, or expanding play episodes. When included in a play environment design, pattern supports consist of a wide variety of storage spots for loose parts and natural materials for collection and expansion of play. Play components that build a sense of place—like a semi-enclosed space—are pattern supports for branching. Providing multiple choices to be used during play facilitates children's natural tendency to use branching behavior and to become fully engaged in the act of playing.

pattern supports for branching
PLAY BEHAVIOR

1. Natural materials like dirt, sand, rocks, stones, water, grasses, bushes or shrubs to play under, twigs, sticks, berries, pine cones, leaves of many shapes and sizes (nonpoisonous)

2. Loose parts provided by adults as part of the daily preparation for play (require easy storage)

3. Simple provisions for imaginative play: play counters, child-sized table and chairs, playhouses, cubbies in which to put things during play

4. Cozy, semi-enclosed spots

One of the best ways to determine whether children are fully engaged in a play episode is to observe the play environment following the play episode. If the children used natural materials or loose parts during play, bunches of leaves or sticks and small stacks of arranged and sorted loose parts are gathered in piles and left in the semi-enclosed places selected for play.

design considerations for
PATTERN SUPPORTS

D UE TO THE REPETITIVE NATURE OF CHILDREN'S PLAY using looping and branching play behaviors, it is necessary for the built characteristics of the play structure and environment to afford a wide diversity and variety of activities. These include structural sensory and movement components, cozy spots and natural materials and/or loose parts that stimulate sensory and/or movement activity during play. Several considerations should be used to direct the design of an ALPHA play environment grouping, or ALPHA PEG.

complexity with an ALPHA PEG

Item #1—Multiple looping pattern supports are provided within the design.

Note: Approximately five children can play successfully in each circuit. If the environment is heavily used, and if the design has overlapping pattern supports, then conflicts can occur between children during play.

Recommendation: Design the ALPHA PEG with a specific number of users in mind and then apply a ratio of one circuit for every five children.

Item #2—A variety of motor and sensory-rich activities is provided.

Note: Do not repeat play components. (Choose different slides, climbers and platform shapes to create circuit.)

Recommendation: Select climbers that are progressive in the climbing skill required to use them, some simple and some more challenging.

Item #3—Provide semi-enclosed ground-level spaces.

Note: Children will prefer these cozy places when they have a child's scale. For supervision, part of the child must be seen from an angle of observation.

Recommendation: Design the ALPHA PEG with a specific number of users in mind and then apply a ratio of one cozy spot for every five children.

Item #4—Abundant play environments reduce play conflicts and enrich the play episode for all children.

Recommendation: Provide multiple play activities and a variety of play events to support the predictable play behaviors of children.

Item #5— Play environments should allow all children, regardless of ability, the opportunity to experience height.

Recommendation: Provide a ramped composite play structure or hill with an accessible pathway.

summary

THE GOAL OF PLAY environment design based on the Boundless Playgrounds play behavior framework is to provide complexity within the play setting. Complexity in a play environment dictates many play choices where children with and without disabilities can use all of the experiences they have acquired to this point and make discoveries that lead to engaged play episodes. These places include far more than just using the play equipment. Children can and will constantly pursue the next experience they need the most to forward their own development. Adults can design complex play environments that are a child's laboratory of discovery and learning.❖

keeping the play EXPERIENCE FRESH

keeping the play EXPERIENCE FRESH

I love to get child stories second-hand. Usually, in the second or third telling, we get all of the details. An associate at Boundless Playgrounds told this story.

Sam is a very handsome boy with an unequalled talent for expressing himself. Like many boys of five years, Sam has acquired a good wooden train collection. The tank engine and all of his friends, and their tracks and other assorted accessories live in Sam's favorite room, the family room, just off the kitchen. Sam's mom, Leslyn, likes to cook and spends a good deal of her after work time in the kitchen where she can also keep an ear on Sam's doings in the family room.

On the way home from work one Friday, Leslyn decided that Sam could have the new tanker he had been asking for, since he had gotten a good report at school that week. Upon arriving at home, new toy in hand, Sam went straight in to play with his trains. Most days it was pretty quiet in the other room. Today, though, was different. All of the trains were talking with loud, deep voices to the new tanker. "You are so heavy!" "Some of the other cars will have to wait while we go over the mountain!" "We will need to rearrange our schedule!"

Curious about what was going on in the train room, Leslyn stood in the doorway watching Sam moving the trains around the track while continuing the debate among the old trains, the new tanker and the cargo cars. Sensing his mother's presence, Sam looked up. Instantly, the trains' conversations halted. Sam looked directly at his mother with a certain indignity written on his face. Leslyn was puzzled by the interruption in play but was more surprised by Sam's frank comment, "Could I have a little privacy here, please?"

Sam became engaged in play quickly because of the new character, the tanker. This small, seemingly insignificant addition to Sam's play generated a whole new and meaningful dimension. When he saw his mother watching him, he felt a need to ensure that he could privately continue his investigation of these new relationships among the train personalities. Small changes in the play setting or minor additions of loose parts empower children to become engaged in play, and these engaged play episodes have developmental benefit for children. Like Sam, all children explore their world through play.

One observation emerges as a compelling aspect of the facilitation of developmentally advantageous outdoor play environments. That observation is related to how children react to the provision of novelty in their play setting. Novelty provides two unique characteristics that are under the exclusive control of adults, particularly within the playground environments of preschool children. One of these characteristics is making minor changes to the outdoor play setting, like changing wind chimes or colored flags that represent the seasons or holidays, or adding new flowers to the planters. The other is rotating the loose parts or toys that are used during children's outdoor play episodes. It is the combination of both of these aspects—minor changes to the play setting and the rotation of loose parts—that constitutes nov'lication.

increasing numbers of objects, on a rotating basis, to create novel relationships in children's imaginations and in their play. The provision of novelty in the environment by an adult facilitator can help children develop skills and abilities across all of the domains of development as quickly as their eager minds allow.

the play attraction continuum IS NOVELTY

AS CHILDREN GROW AND MATURE DURING PLAY, THEY organize and classify their world. Novel occurrences and novel objects introduced into the environment present information for children to learn while doing. The information is used to change how children think and how they actually play.

Their play patterns change from the dominant, repetitive form, looping, into a time of acquiring other objects to manipulate and different patterns to use and include in their play, branching. Children's needs necessitate the availability of

Great care should be given in using novelty as an attractor of children to play. Novelty attracts children to explore and to seek new information in the play setting. Over time, however, the novelty of an object wears off. If the object is lacking in complexity, it is likely that it will no longer be selected for play. If the play equipment that children use daily is a novel themed play structure (i.e., clearly defined castle, boat, rocket ship, etc.), it will attract children's attention for a period of time but will not hold their interest over the months and maybe years that they will use the playground. Novelty in the form of an overt theme on a permanent playground structure is only truly novel to the first-time visitors.

Having said that, novelty is a valuable characteristic of a play setting because it attracts children to play. Most parents have noticed that their young children seem to gravitate toward the newest object even when provided a known, complex environment in which to play. Young children always pick the new object to manipulate in spite of the presence of a favorite toy. This event sheds light on a significant indicator of children's choices during play. When the object is considered new or novel, it will likely be chosen first for play.

Changes in the play environment refresh the novel attraction of the play setting and draw the children in a different way each time changes are made or new loose parts are introduced. The outcome is refreshed play episodes that will take many different turns over the course of repeated play sessions. This variety in play experience is usually the result of the exploration of new combinations of things to learn and do, i.e., novelty.

Novelty in the play environment is the engine that focuses children's attention on new aspects of discovery. As children collect sensory-motor information from different movement experiences and a wide range of manipulative play experiences within the play environment, they store all of this information for classification into groups. These groups of information help children internally organize their worlds.

For example, children collect information when playing in the sand play area with containers used for pouring. The sand is poured from one container to another and back again. The new, stored information is focused on comparative volumes between containers. "Does a short, flat container hold the same amount as the tall, skinny container?" Through repeated trials over time, information about containers, their shapes, and the volume each container holds is stored for the eventual conceptual assembly of the notion of equal volumes, different shapes.

Adult intervention is required to provide the novel elements of play within the play environment to spark the children's interest in their daily play adventures. One simple way to support the predictable play behavior of children and add novelty to the sand play area is to frequently change the sand play toys. Three or four different bins with various types of "stuff" in each bin for use in sand play provide the type of novel change of which we are speaking. Allowing children only a few days of play with the contents of one bin prior to its collection and the provision of another bin's contents is an example of the provision of novelty in a play setting. In other words, rotate the sand play toys frequently. In this way a child's notion of sand pouring is expanded through the repetition of manipulative play and motor activity with different things. This is one of the guidelines for abundance (mentioned in Chapter 4) within a play environment—a large selection of similar things with variations on a theme. The theme in this case is sand play toys. The abundance is delivered by the variety contained in each bin and in the cycling of the bins for use by the children periodically.

supervision—
INTERVENTION OR INTERRUPTION?

ADULT INTERVENTIONS TO PROVIDE NOVELTY WITHIN THE play environment are best achieved covertly. Children seem to take maximum advantage of provisions that they "discover." When adding novel features to the play environment or when supplying the play environment with play supports like the sand toys, add these things to the playground before the children enter. Let them make discoveries on their own. The reward is terrific developmental gains.

As has been discussed throughout this text, children need vast opportunities to be independent and self-directed during play. This need to be uninterrupted during play has huge developmental benefits for children. When they play, new neurological connections are being made. It is possible and maybe probable that if a child is interrupted at a critical point of discovery, that exact point cannot be recreated by the child in a future play episode. Great sensitivity is required by adults observing children during play to avoid interference or interruption. When we hear children speaking, they are not necessarily talking to an adult bystander, nor are they neces-

sarily requesting our assistance. The supervisor's surreptitious actions or their direct interruptions have an affect on the quality of children's play. Surreptitious actions have a positive affect while direct interruption can produce negative results.

There are three types of interruptions that produce differences in the quality of a child's play experience. These interruptions can be caused by other children or by an adult, but since children view adults as authority figures, the interruption caused by an adult may have a more devastating consequential affect. The three types are:

1. **Distraction** - The least consequential interruption of a child's engaged play episode is a distraction – it is only momentary and the child can quickly refocus attention on his play.

2. **Interference** – A moderate hindrance to play, interference is caused by an obstruction or impediment that requires the child to re-route to re-engage in their play episode. For children with attention deficit disorder (ADD) this amount of disturbance may cause a

breakdown in the play episode and reengagement may not be possible.

3. **Disruption** – This is the most significant type of interruption a child will face during an engaged play episode. The child losing complete control of the play episode characterizes a disruption of play. The play episode is thrown into disorder and is broken apart. If the child is on the brink of making a significant connection neurologically as the disruption occurs, this learning opportunity will be lost and might not be recaptured.

It bears repeating that adults should approach the play of children with great sensitivity. During the observation of children at play, do not interfere or interrupt. Whenever possible, allow the child to come to the natural conclusion of the play episode to redirect their activities. These are precious discovery and learning opportunities for *all* children.

Observation of children who incorporate novel play supports into familiar play settings demonstrates the change that does and can occur in patterns of thinking during play. The language children use changes from reciting names and identifying objects, or categories of objects, into the larger conceptual world of comparisons and relationships. That language is about, "She's bigger than he is," or "I'm in front and he's in back." Low and high, front and back, little and big, and things on the side are frequent comparisons made with loose parts found in play settings.

The motor play that takes place on a composite play structure also provides lots of opportunities to make comparisons and discover the relationships between people and other concrete things. This leads to children's ability to build and understand abstract concepts. Children gather observations of one child's position in comparison to the position of another child on the play structure. This helps them place into their abstract classifications ways to define relationships to each other. (Remember Patty from Chapter 1 learning that things have names and things also have color?)

While it is important that adults not interrupt children during play so that they may receive the maximum developmental benefit from the play episode, adult supervision during play is critical to ensure safety. Even the very best playgrounds cannot supervise children during play. Adults must do that. Supervision must be attentive but not intrusive. Adults should give children great liberty during play, only intervening when they are about to hurt themselves or others.

Maintaining an awareness of the child's need to achieve and sustain an engaged play episode can help adults deliver maximum develop-mental benefit during play. It might be helpful to consider some questions when supervising children in the play environment.

When supervising a playground:

1. Am I letting the child have choices in their play?

2. Is the child intrinsically motivated to engage in play or am I making that choice for them?

3. Is my presence supporting or hindering the children's ability to access an imaginative world of play?

4. Am I forcing myself into a play episode or am I waiting to be invited?

5. Have I coached the children on their conduct during play rather than directing or controlling them?

Children should be given latitude during play to explore how their behaviors affect others. Experiencing consequences is one of the best means for a child to learn the nature of self-discipline. Establishing playground rules is one positive way to influence the child. Rules that are positive confirm children as they practice a growing sense of self-discipline during play. These rules should be simply worded and positive in nature. Limit the number of rules for children who play in an ALPHA PEG – three rules work well for the least sophisticated players.

nov'lication within an ALPHA PEG

THE FOLLOWING ARE IDEAS OF HOW AN ALPHA PEG can regularly be refreshed to continuously attract children to productive engaged play.

- Provide a wide variety of loose-parts materials.
  Note: To achieve nov'lication, bins with toys and playthings must be stored in convenient locations near play so that adults can easily make them available to the children on a rotating basis.

- Play props like road signs and tents for creating a village should be available on a rotating basis.

• Be adventurous! Create a water park in the playground by using various hoses and sprinklers in combination for a summertime event. This could be a weeklong project with many groups of children taking different roles.

• Bring the dress-ups outside.

• Build a town with appliance boxes.

• Decorate the playhouse! Make curtains, gather pillows and throw rugs for a whole new play experience.

• Create an adventure maze with straw bales, traffic cones or PVC pipe frames and sheets.

• Use small planters throughout the playground to add seasonal plants and teach the children about plant care.

• Windsocks, wind chimes and small garden sculptures can be rotated in location and changed periodically.

• Play all types of music—marches, classical, popular, standards and jazz.

• Allow the children to create outdoor art with sidewalk chalk, snow painting with colored water or painting sidewalks with water using brushes and rollers of all sizes.

• Keep a large collection of wheeled vehicles. Rotate them for variety during play sessions.
Note: Provide as wide a variety of riders as possible—tricycles with and without pedals, wagons, pedal cars, scooters, plastic riding toys, tractors.

summary

KEEPING THE PLAY ENVIRONMENT FRESH SO THAT IT attracts children to engaged play episodes takes the same type of effort that is required to prepare an instructional lesson. The really big difference is that for the mission to be successful in the outdoor play environment, preparations must be covert. In other words, the children need to independently discover the new elements of the play environment and integrate them into their engaged play episodes. This is a simple yet often overlooked opportunity for adults to expand the developmental benefits of independent, self-directed play for children. ❧

barrier-free is fun FOR EVERYONE

barrier-free is fun FOR EVERYONE

HERE WE ARE! THIS IS THE CHAPTER WITH THE MAGICAL potion! In these pages are all of the answers to the really big questions! This is the chapter that takes the mystery out of accommodations and describes how you can make the play environment a place of independent play for all children. Actually, there is no magical potion—we simply have to think like children.

I had been looking forward to my day with Alyssa for weeks. We had the whole day planned. Starting early on Saturday morning, we were going to visit all of the new playgrounds I had designed in Connecticut. This was a big deal for Alyssa; she had never been on an all-day field trip with anyone outside of her family. We were going to drive to five playgrounds and play on all of them.

With final hugs for Mommy and Daddy, we were on our way. Playground visits one and two were enjoyable. Alyssa, 3½ years old, was in her glory. She had my undivided attention and I had hers. We had fun climbing, sliding, hiding, crawling, laughing, peeking, exploring.

As we walked around our third playground, Alyssa said to me, "Jean, I'm a kid." I responded, "That's right, Alyssa. You're a kid." She wasn't finished with her thought. "And Mommy's she's a dult (an adult)." Seeing her pattern, I agreed. She continued, "And

Daddy's he's a dult." Once again, I agreed. "That's right, Alyssa. Mommy and Daddy are adults." I was very pleased that she had made the connection between generations and children and adults.

What she said next has given me great joy and had a profound impact on my thinking about how we interact with children and how we should design their play environments. Alyssa said, "But, Jean, you a kid, too!"

I may never fully understand what prompted Alyssa's declaration, yet I continue to believe in the possibility that as adults, we can maintain a true childlike quality. It is that childlikeness that will help us plan play environments where all children can find what they want and need for engaged play episodes.

organizing the THINKING

IT SEEMS REDUNDANT AT THIS POINT TO SAY THAT THE most important accommodation the planners of a play environment can provide is the opportunity for *all* children, with and without disabilities to achieve engaged play. This is the goal—to make the play environment a safe place of dignity, independence and self-directed exploration for each child regardless of abilities or disabilities. Within an ALPHA PEG, the activities for play center around gathering

movement and sensory information, which influences
children's development of
the physical/sensory
domain, and figuring out
how the world works by
manipulating things under
their control, which influences
their intellectual development. The
most beneficial accommodations in the playground will relate
to the predictable play behaviors and preeminent domains of
development by providing as much independent play as possible for all children during engaged play episodes.

All children who are
capable of independent
play want three things in
a playground: They want
to do fun things, they
want to be in interesting
places and everybody
wants to be in the middle
of play. This is the essence
of play. It is what makes play compelling for children and
why they are excited about doing it.

Most children are capable of independent play in some
form. Children who have profound disabilities and who

therefore cannot play independently yet, can still enjoy their
playground visits because of the social connections with other
people and the pleasurable sensory stimulation provided.
With this thinking in mind, the play environment should
include play events for all children to explore (independently)
and some play events that provide sensory benefits that may
require caregiver intervention (assistance). Not all of the play
events in a play environment will be useful for all children.
To provide the best environment for all children, the play
environment should include a range of ALPHA PEG play
events and sensory experiences for both children who require
assistance and those who play independently.

As a civil rights law, the Americans
with Disabilities Act states that all
Americans have the right to
access public facilities. Making
the playground accessible is a
requirement of the Americans
with Disabilities Act
Accessibility Guidelines
(ADAAG). Boundless
Playgrounds design philosophy builds on the ADA's
foundation to create play
environments where children
with and without disabilities

Mild   Moderate   Profound

explore an environment supporting their independent self-directed play.

The purpose of this chapter is to provide specific recommendations that will make the playground *play-useful* for all children. Public playgrounds designed for all children should provide accommodations for as many children with disabilities as possible. We have divided the types of disabilities into three broad categories related to the specific needs of children that should be considered during the design of a play environment—mobility impairments, cognitive delays, and sensory dysfunctions. Each of these categories can be addressed with accommodations on the playground that will specifically meet the needs of the children who have these disabilities and at the same time, enhance the play experiences for all children, including children without disabilities.

To further explain the level of accommodation provided for in each disability category, a line graph below each photo in this chapter indicates the accommodation for children within a range in each of these categories. The greatest accommodations are indicated with a star at profound, indicating that the children who are the most profoundly impaired will be able to use this play element in their wheelchairs or with minor assistance from a care provider.

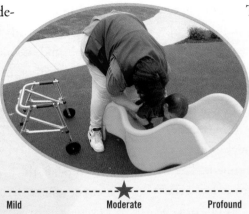

Mild   Moderate   Profound

This approach to play environment design may seem simplistic because it doesn't take into consideration that children may have impairments in more than one category. It has been selected so that specific design suggestions can be addressed in a way that will help adults more and less familiar with various disabilities provide appropriate accommodations. Since each child is an individual with a wide range of unique characteristics, these categories and the indicated ranges cannot be the sole predictor of successful interactions for all children.

mobility IMPAIRMENTS

MOST PLAYGROUNDS WHERE EFFORTS HAVE BEEN MADE to provide play for children with disabilities have focused on providing accommodations for children with mobility impairments. These accommodations include the removal of the architectural barriers that limit where children can play. In Chapter 7, a discussion about the design of pathways and playground safety surfacing is intertwined with the selection of these materials to provide accessible surfaces for children with mobility impairments. The design of surfaces within playgrounds can also provide sensory experiences for the children playing in an ALPHA PEG.

Mild   Moderate   Profound

Once children are in the playground, what can they do? All children who visit an ALPHA PEG are developing their independent mobility skills. All children in the basic play behavior phase need many opportunities to change their body positions and base of support and to practice movement skills. Some children with mild and moderate mobility impairments, although their progress in developing independent mobility skills may be delayed, are excited about the movement challenges that are found in playgrounds. Most children playing in an ALPHA PEG will need to experience many types of movement challenges to hone their skills. Composite play structures with a variety of slides, climbers and connectors like tunnels are advantageous.

All children need to practice changing their body positions. One way to make this fun for everyone is to connect play platforms with climbing and sliding events with tunnels in between. Children playing in an ALPHA PEG are comfortable moving in a creep-

ing posture as well as in an erect walking posture. This design configuration levels the playing field for all children when the play structure surfacing is really accessible. To comply with the Americans with Disabilities Act Accessibility Guidelines (ADAAG), play structures that are configured in this way are limited at 19 play components, and a variety of ground-level activities are required as well. See the ADAAG Final Rule for complete details. (A copy of the ADAAG Final Rule can be found on the accompanying CD-ROM.)

All children need a variety of climbing events where they can experience success. Climbers with the option of full body support are excellent choices for the least sophisticated climbers. They will use only their hands and feet in a prone posture assent until they gain climbing skill. This accommodation of providing for fully body support doesn't preclude the child with more sophisticated climbing skill from using the climber in an equally effective manner.

To practice movement skills, all children need a variety of climbing events on their play structures. When selecting the climbing events, consider the movement

Mild   Moderate   Profound

patterns required to successfully maneuver on each event. A good rule to follow is not to repeat climbing events in the ALPHA PEG.

Cozy spots are compelling to all children. A ground-level cozy spot is a true treasure for children with mobility impairments because this is a play place where they can be independent in a child-sized space. This gives children who are otherwise most often very closely monitored by adults an opportunity to experience some liberty during play.

Mild   Moderate   Profound

The first dynamic in creating a cozy spot is the size of the space. It should have at least a 60-inch-diameter area. (This is the minimum turning radius for a child using a wheelchair.) If the area has an opening to enter, make it at least 36 inches wide. Minimum headroom for any opening or roof for a cozy spot should be not less than 48 inches. Each cozy spot should always have at least one interesting thing to do.

Mild   Moderate   Profound

All types of movement can be fun and provide pleasurable sensory experiences. Swings with back supports and extra straps allow children of all abilities the chance to enjoy the fun of swinging. These swings provide the most accommodation when coupled with unitary rubber ground surfacing as shown here. Often these swings are very popular with children without disabilities.

On a beautiful fall day, I went to a Boundless Playgrounds project. There, I was saddened to see a little girl in a wheelchair at the end of a line of three children who were waiting to use the support swing that had a high back and armrests that made it possible for children with disabilities to use it. The other swings in that area were all empty! Everyone wanted to use the special swing!

As I watched, I was torn by my desire to make things right for the little girl at the end of the line, to tell the children without disabilities that they needed to let her go first. After all, they could use any of the swings, and the girl at the end of the line could only use that swing. I wanted to intervene but wasn't sure if I should. And what if I embarrassed the little girl who was using the wheelchair? I wrestled with my emotions for few more minutes and finally started to walk in the little girl's direction.

Just as I was about to say something, the mother of the little girl pulled me aside, out of listening range of all of the children, and said in no uncertain terms that Sarah needed to be treated just like the other children, that learning to share and take turns was as important for her as it was for children without disabilities, and that it was wonderful that the other children thought the special swing was so special that they were

Mild ---- Moderate ---- ★ Profound

willing to wait for a turn while other swings were standing idle. I sat on a nearby bench with this wise mom and watched the children play. The special swings were essential for the children with disabilities but also made children without disabilities feel safe and secure so they weren't afraid to swing. It was a beautiful sight. And while she was waiting, Sarah talked to the other children in line....

Mild ---- ★ Moderate ---- Profound

• Spring riders can be supplied with back supports and foot supports for the children who need additional help with maintaining their position on a play event.

• Playing with different types of materials, like sand and water, are sensory experiences that attract children in the basic play behavior phase when these materials are available for their

use. Children in the transitional play behavior phase also like to play with these materials. As they manipulate sand and water with other loose parts, they master how the world works through their self-directed experiments. A sand and water table with an accessible surface is play-useful for all children.

• All ground-level play features in an ALPHA PEG should provide play-usefulness for children with mobility impairments. Therefore, a unitary rubber surface should be provided to facilitate play in the use zone around playground equipment.

• In the design of play structures with ramps, from a safety standpoint, slides should not start from a play platform where children in wheelchairs could roll off. In adding a transfer point before each slide, two advantages are gained:

Mild ---- Moderate ---- ★ Profound

(1) children using wheelchairs can't inadvertently get their leading wheels headed down the slide and (2) the

Mild   ★ Moderate   Profound

cognitive DELAYS

AS IS TRUE FOR OTHER CHILDREN, PLAY IS A KEY TO development for children with cognitive delays. The more opportunities they are given to explore and observe, the more successfully they will build the neurological frameworks that are responsible for the development of intelligence. The repetitive play activities that are observed during the basic and transitional play behavior phases may endure into middle childhood for children with cognitive challenges. If these play activities are self-directed and independent, children should be given opportunities to continue these play episodes until they are satisfied and independently move on to other activities.

slide is play-useful for children as they transfer from their wheelchair or other support device to the slide.

• To provide maximum developmental benefit for all children, a ramped play structure allows all children regardless of ability the opportunity to experience height. Being up high and viewing the world from a greater vista helps children develop their perspective. With the chance to see all sides of their play environment from one spot, children formulate a fuller understanding of space and the relationships of the places they are familiar with. This is a fundamental building block for many physical and spatial understandings.

• Supervision of children with cognitive delays is a careful balance of allowing the freedom necessary for exploration while intervening prior to the children experiencing serious or harmful consequences for their actions. To facilitate good supervision, the play environment and the playground equip-

Mild   ★ Moderate   Profound

ment must offer clear sight lines. Most children who will play in an ALPHA PEG are able to correctly judge their skill level against a play event, like a climber, to determine their likelihood of success. Children with cognitive delays may need additional coaching or direction to make the most appropriate choices as they develop their movement and decision-making skills.

• Children playing in an ALPHA PEG are predictably less skilled at sharing. It is recommended that popular play events like slides and manipulative play panels be provided in multiples and designed so that the use patterns don't overlap. This design method also applies to play features like steering wheels and cozy seating areas. Children of all abilities benefit from the design approach where an abundance of play features are available for use during engaged play episodes.

• Size and shapes are difficult concepts to master without many opportunities to interact with physical space that gives concrete examples of these concepts. As discussed in earlier chapters, all children are interested in comparisons and relationships.

• To enhance the play environment so that children with cognitive impairments can master comparisons and relationships, provide high places and low, places to crawl

through that are long and places that are short, big spaces to discover and tiny spaces to creep into. A variety of cozy spots mentioned in the mobility impairment category are supportive in the development of the concept associated with comparisons and relationships. During these individual explorations of size and space, most children begin using self-talk that is part of their language acquisition.

• Some children may find the very activities that they have been directed to practice in a physical therapy session very engaging in the playground. One example of a skill

Mild   Moderate   Profound

often directed in therapy is balancing. When balancing components are linked together to form a repetitive sequence as suggested in the pattern support chapter, children will use this playground equipment to master movement skills because it matches their interest in doing loops!

sensory DYSFUNCTION

CHILDREN WITH SENSORY IMPAIRMENTS MAY need to be introduced to a new play environment so that they can feel comfortable about exploring independently. This introduction should include a comprehensive walk around the perimeter where the children are allowed to touch the natural materials like bushes, trees and flowers. They need to understand that these plants and other materials are in the playground for their use during play.

All of the freestanding play features should be located and each piece introduced so that the children understand how the equipment moves. A walk around and through the composite play structure is also appropriate. Show the children where things are that move or make sounds. Playgrounds can have many different sensations underfoot. These changes can serve as a prompt to watch out for swings.

Mild   Moderate   Profound

The play environment should be rich with textures, smells, movement, sounds and sights that are engaging and intriguing.

- To aid in the discrimination of different platform heights on the composite play structure, platforms that are adjacent to one another and different heights should be of contrasting dark and light colors to provide visual differentiation.

- Protective barriers should be located at every opening for stairs and climbers on all platforms that are accessible to children who use wheelchairs. These barriers should

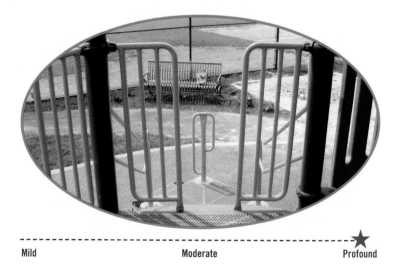

Mild   Moderate   Profound

limit the opening to 15 inches maximum to prevent inadvertent falls. By limiting the opening size, children with all types of disabilities can play with greater liberty because a potential risk for injury has been eliminated. (Neither the *ASTM Standards*, published by the American Society of Testing and Materials, a society of manufacturers and consumer advocates that develops voluntary product safety standards, nor the *CPSC Handbook for Public Playground Safety*, published by the U.S. Consumer Product Safety Commission [publication #325], requires this protective barrier at all openings.)

• A fence with a single opening is a reasonable way to limit the explorations of children in an ALPHA PEG to the area that has been designated for play. Children of all abilities in these first two play phases have a tendency to wander during play. For children with sensory impairments, the fence offers a sense of security.

• Children who have cochlear implants are often advised to refrain from using plastic slides due to the potential for an electro-static discharge (ESD). If an ESD event should occur, the "map-

ping" in the processor could be erased. This would cause the child to again be unhearing until the mapping could be reinstalled. Therefore, it is recommended that each ALPHA PEG have at least one non-plastic slide and if that slide is a metal sliding surface, it should be shaded or a coated roller slide.

• Shade must be a consideration in warm climates. For some children, exposure to the sun can be detrimental to their health due to medical conditions or medications. To provide for these children, some part of the ALPHA PEG should be shaded by trees or with shade structures. Roofs on the play structures can provide part of the equation.

• Some children will need places to isolate themselves during play when the excitement of the play environment becomes overwhelming. The cozy spots may provide this separation from the overpowering sensory overload that a child may experience in a playground. Design a few cozy spots that are "supervisable" yet create a sense of privacy.

Mild   Moderate   Profound

summary

THE FIRST STEP IN THE PROCESS OF designing inclusive play environments is the willingness to see play as the liberty that should be given to every child. Children with disabilities are more like children without disabilities than we tend to think. Clearing the obstacles to play is the work of adults so that children can become engaged in play. This chapter has provided direction toward designing environments where every child is treated with dignity and equal concern for his or her developmental pursuits. We can do no less than the best for our most valuable assets.

Remember, each of the accommodations mentioned in this chapter will greatly enrich the play experiences all children who play in the ALPHA PEG. ✤

Mild   Moderate   Profound

CHAPTER SEVEN

tackling the SITE DETAILS

tackling the SITE DETAILS

Matthew first met Amy Barzach and the other people working to build the Jonathan's Dream playground in West Hartford, CT when he was a charming seven year old boy, smart in every conceivable way with a few missing teeth. Unlike the other children in his class at the Willard School, Matthew couldn't play on the playground at recess with his friends. Matthew has used a power wheelchair to zoom himself around since he was 4 years old. All of the playgrounds in the communities near Matthew's home weren't friendly for children with mobility impairments.

As part of the design process for Jonathan's Dream, Matthew participated in a Dreaming and Design Party where children of all abilities use an array of art supplies and construction toys to express their ideas about what should be in the playground. From the beginning, Matthew was focused on the things all children enjoy doing. He came up with a boat swing. "All children like to pretend that they are sailing a boat and all children like to swing." This boat swing needed to be large enough so that several people could use it together. The boat swing became a play feature at Jonathan's Dream. The best thing about the boat swing is that Matthew can make it move by himself by moving his wheelchair back and forth.

After Jonathan's Dream opened in October 1996, Matthew, William (Matthew's younger brother), and their parents, David and Susan, would often spend afternoons at the playground. Susan was accustomed to following Matthew around other playgrounds to provide assistance. But this was a different kind of place to play – this was a place without barriers where play activities were arranged so that everyone can get engaged in play. Matthew enjoyed the liberty of making his own choices about where he wanted to go and what he wanted to do. One day, feeling very confident that he could manage for himself in this special play environment, Matthew announced to his mother, "Mommy, go sit down, I can do this myself!"

What an amazing realization for Matthew! A child can and should be at liberty to independently explore play environments during play episodes. Several child and adult factors must be in place for all children to discover the liberty that Matthew experienced at Jonathan's Dream. It should be the goal of the adults involved in the development of a playground to anticipate both the needs of children and adults. Also, we assume a certain responsibility for safe and positive experiences within the play environments we design and oversee.

This chapter is about the details that make playgrounds places of freedom and discovery for children including making them barrier-free. These are details that make a difference in how children and families will use playgrounds. In this general information that is critical to the design of a child-focused integrated playground, topics include surfacing, shade, plantings, signage and sight lines so that adults can provide appropriate playground supervision.

surfacing

THE ELEMENTS THAT WILL MOST AFFECT THE PLAY-usefulness and accessibility of a finished play area for all children are the pathways throughout and around the play environment and the resilient safety surfacing material(s) in the use zones around the playground equipment. These "surfaces" can be the playground's best unnoticed asset for

providing a barrier-free, universally accessible play environment. There are many factors that should be considered when selecting the materials for the "surfacing". Consideration should be given to how the materials will be connected throughout the environment including how the playground equipment is integrated into the overall play environment design.

How can the surfacing elements be more important than the selection of play equipment or any of a multitude of other details relating to the overall design and usefulness of an integrated play environment? The answer is at your feet! When a child cannot get onto the playground equipment or is prevented from moving from one area to another due to an uneven surface connection or an inaccessible surface, the entire playground becomes a less valuable asset. Improper combinations of surfacing materials or

A common oversight—an accessible path, which is not connected to the playground.

poor construction details can become the chasm that prevents a child with a mobility impairment from playing with other children in a playground. Pathway and playground use zone surfacing materials must be selected with care so that the transition from one type of surfacing material to another material doesn't present a barrier or a hazard for a child using a wheelchair or other mobility device.

Understanding how these materials interact during use will be helpful when making the decision of which materials to select for the accessible pathways and for resilient safety surfacing material(s) in the use zones around your playground equipment. This chapter will help with the understanding of factors that should govern surfacing decisions:

1. Pathway materials and the design of circulation paths to provide sensory/motor experiences like tricycle tracks,

2. The selection of resilient safety surfacing material(s) in the use zones around the playground equipment, and

3. Placement and layout of resilient safety surfacing materials.

pathways

THE FIRST NECESSARY DETAIL IN DESIGNING a barrier-free, universally accessible playground is to connect a "handicapped accessible parking area" or public walkway to the accessible pathway that leads to the playground. All public pathways must have these characteristics to be accessible. Pathways must meet the following criteria:

1. Be firm, stable and slip-resistant,

2. Be at least 60" wide,

3. Each section of the pathway must not exceed a grade of 1' of rise to each 20' of run, and

4. Wheel stops or curbs must be provided, where necessary, to prevent children using wheelchairs from accidentally leaving the pathway.

The most suitable materials for accessible pathways are poured concrete or asphalt (smooth, pebble finish, scored or stamped with designs - colored or natural), pavers (brick, natural stone, interlocking pavers or "contribution" engraved bricks) or compacted stone dust. Each of these materials has a cost that varies depending on playground location. Some of these materials may have a longer service life depending on weather, flow of surface water and natural vegetation growing

around and up through the pathway. When selecting these surfaces consider adding texture and/or color. Children are gathering sensory information while they are playing, which is important to their development.

Materials that are not acceptable for accessible pathways are any loose materials like sand, gravel, pea stone, rice stone, or river rock. These materials are not firm and stable. Pathways are not considered accessible if undeveloped with grass, compacted soil or clay. In addition, these materials are not slip resistant.

When designing an ALPHA PEG, circulation pathways within the play environment can serve a dual purpose – they will also be used as tricycle tracks. If an ALPHA PEG has a tricycle track it should at least form a simple loop. To increase the complexity of the play environment consider including intersections which form multiple loops, bridges, and small hills. The combination of an interesting path, textures on the path, and cozy spots for imaginative interludes will pay rich dividends in hours of engaged play episodes.

The assistance of a local landscape architect should be obtained to make the best decisions about pathway materials. Technical layout of the pathways and the method to be used when connecting to other existing accessible walkways and parking areas are readily achieved with help of design professionals.

resilient safety SURFACING MATERIALS

THE U.S. CONSUMER PRODUCT SAFETY COMMISSION (USCPSC) provides "The Handbook for Public Playground Safety", at no charge. A copy of the handbook can be obtained by calling the USCPSC at (800) 638-2772. In this document you will find a list of the general categories of resilient safety surfacing materials and their qualities - both advantages and disadvantages. The content of this chapter builds on the information provided in Section 4- "Surfacing" of the USCPSC handbook.

There are three general categories of surfacing materials: organic loose materials, inorganic loose materials and unitary synthetic materials. With focus on their beneficial characteristics, each of these materials can be used to great advantage within the integrated play environment.

Due to their nature of being loose, organic loose materials and inorganic loose materials are difficult to maintain as accessible surfaces according to Americans with Disabilities Act Accessibility Guidelines (ADAAG). Yet, when children fall on these surfaces the material tends to move on impact, providing cushioning to the child's long bones and head. For active play areas with climbing and upper body devices and where falls to the surface can be readily predicted, these materials may be preferable when used in combination with unitary synthetic materials described below.

Unitary synthetic materials are resilient safety surfacing materials that provide excellent accessibility around and through the playground. Two types of these materials are common: (1) tiles and (2) poured in place. These materials are also an impact attenuating surface appropriate for the use zone around playground equipment. Unitary poured in place surface materials are available in a wide range of colors and can be installed with interesting designs. Although this material has a high initial cost, over the lifetime of this surface, the lower requirement for rigorous routine maintenance makes it a viable selection within public play spaces.

Since all of these materials have a variety of benefits, more than one material within the use zones of the play equipment should be considered during the selection of impact attenuating surfacing materials. Some materials (like organic and inorganic loose materials) within the use zones may limit accessibility but may also provide an additional margin of fall safety. Children with mobility impairments may not be using some upper body devices or climbers so the surfacing materials around some of these play components can be selected based on the best choices for a falling surface.

placement AND LAYOUT

WITHIN THE USE ZONES AROUND PLAY EQUIPMENT A further consideration must be made about "play-usefulness". If the surfacing in an area is barrier-free, what play activities are available for all of the children to use? Play-usefulness occurs when the design of the playground equipment, the pathways and the impact attenuating surfacing materials work together to achieve real play opportunities for all children.

The accessible pathways should lead directly to accessible surfaces within the play environment use zone or the entrance to a ramp on a composite play structure. The liberty of all children

Design, Selection, and Relationship of Equipment Components

Planned Pathways that Lead to the Components for Their Use

Impact Attenuating Surfacing to Protect Children during Use

PLAY USEFULNESS
Foundation for Fully Integrated Play

during play must include play experiences at the ground level within the use zone. It should also include opportunities to experience height: for example, a higher view of the surroundings. The surfacing must provide all children with cozy spots: for example, beneath a composite play structure or under the roof on a composite play structure. These are interesting places to be and can provide real independent, self-directed play experiences for all children.

A major concern when designing a universally accessible environment is the provision that all children be in the middle of play. To accomplish this goal, it is not necessary to cover the entire play environment with a unitary synthetic material. In an ALPHA PEG, unitary synthetic material surrounding the composite play structure is preferable to maximize the play-usefulness. At minimum, use this material to connect the accessible routes to the cozy spots and to the sliding and climbing activities on the composite play structure. Placing play activities adjacent to one another with this material economizes the cost while extending the play-usefulness. It cannot be overstated that strategic planning of the playground equipment, the pathways and the surfacing is required to ensure that all variables are considered together.

Surfacing Summary

These guidelines are useful for making surfacing a play asset when planning play environments for all children:

1. Select pathway materials and finishes that provide interesting sensory experiences.

2. More than one type of surfacing material within the use zones of the play equipment should be selected since each type of surfacing has pros and cons related to safety, accessibility and maintenance.

3. All accessible pathways should lead to accessible surfaces or to the entrance to a ramp on a composite play structure.

4. Provide accessible surfaces to interesting places throughout the play environment— consider high places and cozy spots.

5. Plan for play-usefulness with the placement of impact attenuating surfacing materials that match the children's use in each play area.

shade

THERE ARE TWO WAYS TO PROVIDE SHADE WITHIN A playground: natural and constructed. If the playground doesn't have mature trees prior to construction, fast growing trees should be part of the original plan so that in a few years the trees will provide great shade.

When designing a play environment with existing trees— before playground construction begins— assess the health of

the trees and remove any trees that are failing. Some trees may be unacceptable within a play setting because of the type of debris and the volume of debris they produce. An example of one tree that may be unacceptable for use within a play setting is a Sweet Gum tree. This tree drops a round seed pod that has woody spikes. Fruit trees in the core of a playground would be unadvisable since they attract bees and wasps. Some trees that deposit debris may be appealing since the material can be used for play. Local professionals can help with the selection of trees for shade and play. (To ensure the long-term health of the trees follow the recommendations of local professionals for maintenance and pruning.)

If the natural shade of a tree is not possible shade from other sources will help. On a composite play structure a roof can offer shade. Large umbrella style structures can be used to shade a small play feature area. Several playground equipment producers have

structures that are designed to cover entire play areas with cool shade. Cost may be a consideration with these products so add this item to the budget if building shade structures is a factor.

Another choice for making the play environment cooler is misters. These are water features that spray a fine water mist on demand. Plumbing is required and installation over a hard surface is recommended.

plantings

NATURALLY GROWING THINGS ARE VERY interesting to children. They love to discover how plants change during the seasons. Children also enjoy nurturing plants. Many of the children in the stories throughout this book have used natural materials – parts of plants – to engage in play. It seems rational and consistent with the predictable play behaviors of children for a play setting to provide maximum play benefit that there must be plants. If the children will be harvesting leaves, sticks, berries, nuts, pine cones, and grasses, there must be a ready supply of them somewhere nearby for the children during play.

The materials that are selected for inclusion in the play setting should be hearty. Some plants like to be defoliated dur-

ing the growing season. They react with more growth as a result of the pruning.

The best selections for the play setting will be plants that are indigenous to the region. These plants are native because they are adapted to the prevailing conditions and will require very little routine maintenance. (To insure the long-term health of the landscaping, follow the recommendations of local professionals for maintenance, irrigation, and pruning.) The other child-focused benefit for using native plant materials is that the children will learn more about these plants by playing with them. As the children mature these plants that are common to them from their childhood will foster their respect for other natural living things.

Lastly, all of the plant materials selected for use within a play setting must be non-poisonous. Care should be given to excluding plants that have known allergens. When child-friendly materials are selected, following the recommendations of local professionals, the play environment can support the predictable play behaviors of children. When feasible use raised planting beds in the play environment so that the plants are within the reach range of children with mobility impairments (between 14" and 18" high).

Plants will be used by children for play, but landscaping in a playground provides more rich benefits than just making it a beautiful place. Shrubs and hedges can form interesting cozy spots. A row of bushes or boulders can be used to separate a busy part of the playground from the quiet sand play area or to give a visual edge to the swing area. When planning a playground for many groups of children, landscaping can give each area a distinctive personality, where a real sense of place can emerge.

fences

THE SECURITY OF A PLAYGROUND IS IMPORTANT. THE easiest way to provide a secure perimeter is with a fence. Whether its purpose is to keep the children within a prescribed area or to limit uninvited guests, a fence should be selected based on the intended objective. This is another playground site feature where the qualified recommendations of a local professional are helpful. Consider the service life, routine maintenance requirements, climb-ability and aesthetics in the decision. In childcare facilities state licensing requirements may be authoritative.

Gates within the fence should be located to accommodate pedestrian traffic. If gates are secured with a lock, be sure that all staff members are trained with lock operation or are aware of the location of the keys. Plan the fence and the gates for emergency evaluation of injured children and for routine maintenance of the playground equipment and surfaces.

signage

IN PLAY ENVIRONMENTS WHERE CHILDREN ARE CLOSELY supervised by a trained staff it may seem superfluous to post signs about the appropriateness of play environments for certain groups of children. The American Society for Testing and Materials has taken the position that in the interest of safety, a sign should be post in every playground indicating for which age of children the playground has been designed. This is a voluntary product safety standard but it is commonly accepted with the U.S. Consumer Product Safety Commission (USCPSC) "The Handbook for Public Playground Safety", as the standard of care. Therefore it is recommended that all play environments designed in compliance with the ALPHA PEG approach be age-rated for children 2 to 5 years, and that signs be prominently posted to advise all users of the playground.

sight lines and the placement OF ADULT SEATING

IN PLANNING FOR A SAFE PLAYGROUND, THE needs of the adult supervisors must be a priority. After all, the only way for children to be truly safe in a play environment is while under the supervision of an adult. The children in an ALPHA PEG are still learning about cause and effect; they still are somewhat unreliable predictors of outcomes. Therefore, adults must be available to intercede before children injure themselves.

The design phase of a playground is the ideal time to deal with one of the most difficult aspects of playground supervision – blind spots! Early in the project determine if there are existing blind spots on the playground site and plan the location of play events so that adults can see all of the children during play. Buildings, storage units, trees, shrubs and playground equipment itself can create blind spots on a playground. Careful planning of the playground can insure that these natural and man-made features are assets on the playground.

Establishing good sightlines from various strategically placed spots can help the supervising staff. Good sight lines are a combination of placement of play features, so that view across the play environment is not restricted, and selecting playground equipment that allows for continuous viewing of some part of the children no matter where they are on the play equipment.

If the playground is to be used by families and the primary supervision will be provided by parents, be sure to consider their comfort while visiting the playground with their children. Benches should be located so that there is a clear sightline through the playground and of the play equipment. Shade is a must. If a parent can't find a comfortable place to sit while children are engaged in play, the visit will be short. Select benches with comfort in mind. Backs and arm rests are preferable. When possible, group benches in pairs so that parents can enjoy conversation while watching their children play.

maintenance

SOMETIMES THE MOST IMPORTANT POINTS ARE THE LAST ones discussed. In the unfortunate event that a child is injured on the playground, the maintenance of the equipment and the procedures followed for maintenance will be considered as evidence of good intention to provide a safe environment for the children. As the new playground is completed, an audit should be completed by a knowledgeable professional called a Certified Playground Safety Inspector (CPSI). The National Recreation and Parks Association (NRPA) administers the program to train and certify playground safety inspectors (To contact the NRPA to find a local CPSI - 22377 Belmont Ridge Road Ashburn, VA 20148-4501 - (703) 858-0784 or www.nrpa.org). The audit documents and establishes a baseline for all future assessments of the safety of the playground. Children will enjoy the long term benefits of a well designed playground, if that playground has the tender attention that comes from a well conceived and executed routine maintenance plan. These are the characteristics of a good maintenance plan.

Begin by creating a detailed inventory of the playground equipment, including: site layout, date of purchase/installation, manufacturer, installation contractor. Photographs of each piece of equipment should be attached to this equipment description. The manufacturer's documentation about the piece

of equipment should also be attached. The manufacturer's documentation should include: installation instructions, recommended routine maintenance guidelines and procedures, and replacement parts list.

Each item on the playground should also have an easy-to-use maintenance diary. Utilizing the manufacturer's recommendations, a list of tasks and frequency of the tasks can be established. These diaries should include the dates of routine maintenance, the dates and reasons for preventative maintenance, and the dates and reasons for remedial maintenance (maintenance preformed as a result of vandalism). The owner/operator of the play environment is responsible to maintain these records and should store them in a central location.

summary

A FULLY INTEGRATED, BARRIER-FREE, DEVELOPMENTALLY advantageous play environment is much more than play components arranged over a soft surface. Attention paid to the site details can mean the difference between children of all abilities having developmentally beneficial play opportunities and a play environment with good intentions that inadvertently has barriers in the layout that inhibits the access for all users. Let's look at several recommendations for tackling the site details.

Surfacing:

- Make sure an accessible route of travel is laid out from the site access/egress point to the play equipment area. The path should be constructed so that the surface is firm, stable and slip resistant.

- Select materials and finishes for the accessible routes that will maximize the sensory experiences for all users.

- Provide a variety of surfacing types that will be contained within the use zones of the play environment. Surfacing choices should account for initial budget, maintenance needs, safety of the play activities and accessibility.

- Consider the "play-usefulness" of the surfacing in relation to the arrangement and layout of the play equipment. Maximize the opportunities to gain access to areas of integrated play, such as cozy spots, while economizing the cost of materials needed to carry out those aims.

Site Amenities:

- Look for ways to provide shade within the play environment. Natural elements and constructed features can create the desired shade for the play environment.

- Utilize water or mist as a means to enhance the play experiences of all users. In addition to cooling off users on a hot day, water play is also beneficial for generating a wide range of sensory experiences.

- Comfortable seating should also be provided in a play environment. Benches should have backs and arm rests and be arranged to foster interaction between the users. Also, consider benches scaled for children to comfortably use and enjoy.

- A storage system, like a shed, for loose parts is an asset within the play environment. Play materials that are provided at the beginning of the play session and collected at the end of play will need to be stored.

Plant Materials:

- Provide a variety of plant materials that are hardy and provide interest throughout the year. Consider texture, height and fragrance and placing plants in locations where all users can enjoy their attributes.

- Select plants so that children can incorporate twigs, leaves, fruit or flowers into their play. Consult a local landscape architect, botanist, master gardener or horticulturalist to ensure plant choices are free of toxins or other irritants if ingested or come into contact with the users.

- Arrange the plant materials to create a space that generates ambience or sense of place for all users.

Fences:

- Provide a means to secure the play environment from either children inadvertently leaving the space or as a way to limit uninvited guests.

- Consideration for the design and layout of a fence should be given to aesthetics, maintenance requirements and life expectancy for the materials selected. Consult with a local professional.

- Gates should be provided for secure but easy access and also account for maintenance and/or service vehicles.

Signage:

- It is recommended that a sign be posted that indicates the age of children for which the play equipment was intended.

- Signs should be simple to read, provide contact information of the owner/operator and incorporate creativity to get the message across.

Supervision:

- Supervision should be a consideration for the design and layout of a play environment.

- There should be clear sight lines through key areas of the play components so supervisors, care givers or parents can quickly and easily locate the users without interfering in their independent play.

- Location and comfortable places to sit are important factors to consider so that adults are available to intercede before a child injures themselves.

Maintenance:

- It is recommended that allocating resources for ongoing maintenance of the play environment is essential for longevity and to keep the components functioning properly.

- Develop a list of maintenance tasks to be performed and their frequency needed to ensure the safety of the play environment. This should be documented on an easy-to-use form that is stored in a central location.

- Create a site history for the play environment complete with a scaled plan of the site, photographs, manufacturer's contact information, date of purchase/installation, and a detailed list of play components. ❧

sample DESIGNS

sample DESIGNS

WHY INCLUDE THIS CHAPTER? THE GOAL WAS TO CREATE a tool, a layperson's handbook, to support the development of new playgrounds and to influence the renovation of existing ones. Our intent was to provide an inclusive resource that would help people create play environments where *all* children could experience the benefits of independent, self-directed, engaged play. We wanted to make it easy for people who love children to give children the best environments for play.

First, the underlying assumptions were identified. Next, a framework for thinking about how children play in outdoor environments was provided followed by suggestions on how to address the built environment. Since ever-changing play environments are more stimulating for children, methods to achieve this objective were included. Finally, details about accommodations for children of all abilities and site construction details were described.

As an unbiased, knowledgeable but neutral nonprofit organization, the National Center for Boundless Playgrounds has successfully collaborated with most national, and a growing number of regional play equipment manufacturers on playground projects. Manufacturers were invited to participate in this book to provide a visual representation of the concepts presented in *High Expectations, Early Childhood*

Edition. Boundless Playgrounds appreciates their commitment to play environments where children of all abilities can play and learn together. We hope you will consider using these product examples as you develop or renovate your play environments. These product advertorials provide "proof" that every play environment can be developmentally advantageous, no matter who makes the equipment.

Boundless Playgrounds believes that there are three essential characteristics of play environments that give children of all abilities the best opportunity to participate in engaged play. The three significant play environment attributes and their importance to children during play were described in detail in Chapter 4 and Chapter 6. These characteristics are:

1. The play features and components are selected to be developmentally appropriate then arranged so that their configuration supports children's predictable play behaviors and provides play-useful accommodations.

2. Cozy spots are child-sized and equipped with play features to reflect the characteristics of children's predictable play behaviors.

3. The play environment provides the experience of height to give all children a growing understanding of relationship and space. Every child, with or without disabilities, is able to get to and play on the highest play platform centers.

When present in a playground, each of these significant play environment attributes will add to the overall benefits for children. Each of these characteristics is valuable. In a play environment where *all* three characteristics are present, children will engage in play episodes that are the most developmentally advantageous.

The following advertorial portion of this publication has been provided by industry manufacturers. An effort was made to be inclusive by inviting members of leading industry associations to participate. If you know of other manufacturers who should be invited to participate in future *Boundless Playgrounds* publications, please have them contact www.boundlessplaygrounds.org or call 860-243-8315.

Editors Note: The authors reviewed advertorial contained in *High Expectations, Early Childhood Edition* according to established criteria and guidelines. The objective was to support public awareness of commercially available products and to avoid advertisements that might confuse the reader. Acceptance of advertorial in *High Expectations, Early Childhood Edition* should not be construed, however, as an endorsement by the authors or the National Center for Boundless Playgrounds. The authors and *Boundless Playgrounds* did not test advertised products and therefore, cannot ensure their safety and efficacy. Acceptance of advertorial does not imply that the authors or the *National Center for Boundless Playgrounds* have conducted an independent scientific review to validate product safety and efficacy or advertising claims.

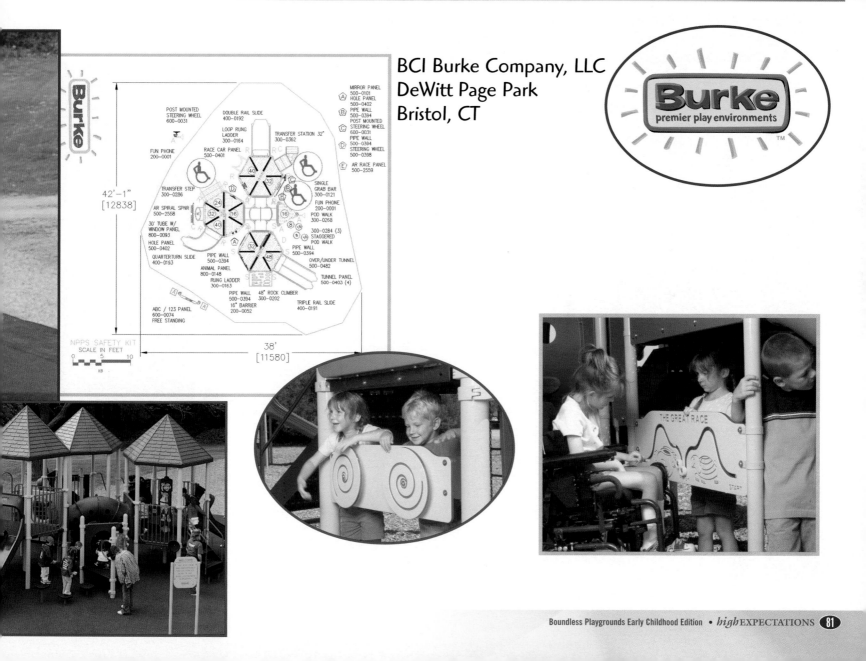

BCI Burke Company, LLC
DeWitt Page Park
Bristol, CT

Burke
premier play environments
™

MIRROR PANEL
500-0101
(A) HOLE PANEL
500-0402
(B) PIPE WALL
500-0394
(C) POST MOUNTED
STEERING WHEEL
600-0031
(D) PIPE WALL
500-0394
STEERING WHEEL
500-0398
(E) AR RACE PANEL
500-2559

DOUBLE RAIL SLIDE
400-0192

POST MOUNTED
STEERING WHEEL
600-0031

LOOP RUNG
LADDER
300-0164

TRANSFER STATION 32"
300-0362

RACE CAR PANEL
500-0401

FUN PHONE
200-0001

SINGLE
GRAB BAR
300-0121

FUN PHONE
200-0001

POD WALK
300-0268

300-0284 (3)
STAGGERED
POD WALK

TRANSFER STEP
300-0286

AR SPIRAL SPNR
500-2558

30' TUBE W/
WINDOW PANEL
800-0093

HOLE PANEL
500-0402

QUARTERTURN SLIDE
400-0193

ANIMAL PANEL
800-0148

RUNG LADDER
300-0163

PIPE WALL
500-0394

PIPE WALL
500-0394

OVER/UNDER TUNNEL
500-0482

TUNNEL PANEL
500-0403 (4)

PIPE WALL
500-0394

48" ROCK CLIMBER
300-0202

TRIPLE RAIL SLIDE
400-0191

16" BARRIER
200-0052

ABC / 123 PANEL
600-0074
FREE STANDING

42'-1"
[12838]

38'
[11580]

NPPS SAFETY KIT
SCALE IN FEET
0   5   10

THE SISKIN CHILDREN'S INSTITUTE

The kids at Siskin love the new experiences they discover while at play!

The accessible playground at Siskin resulted in a lab partnership between the institute and GameTime. New products can be tested at the school, and evaluated for accessibility, play value and compliance.

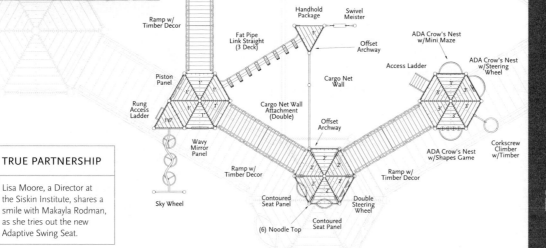

TRUE PARTNERSHIP

Lisa Moore, a Director at the Siskin Institute, shares a smile with Makayla Rodman, as she tries out the new Adaptive Swing Seat.

NEW!
POWER SCAPE PLUS

LAKE WATERFORD PARK

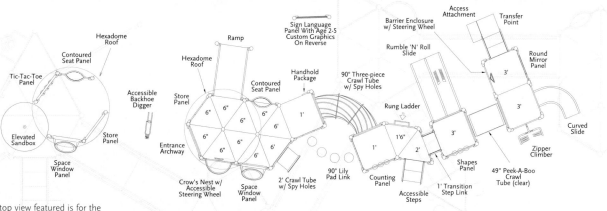

Tic-Tac-Toe Panel
Contoured Seat Panel
Hexadome Roof
Ramp
Sign Language Panel With Age 2-5 Custom Graphics On Reverse
Access Attachment
Transfer Point
Barrier Enclosure w/ Steering Wheel
Rumble 'N' Roll Slide
Round Mirror Panel
Accessible Backhoe Digger
Hexadome Roof
Store Panel
Handhold Package
Contoured Seat Panel
90° Three-piece Crawl Tube w/ Spy Holes
Rung Ladder
Store Panel
Elevated Sandbox
Entrance Archway
Space Window Panel
Crow's Nest w/ Accessible Steering Wheel
Space Window Panel
2' Crawl Tube w/ Spy Holes
90° Lily Pad Link
Counting Panel
Accessible Steps
1' Transition Step Link
Shapes Panel
49" Peek-A-Boo Crawl Tube (clear)
Zipper Climber
Curved Slide

6" 6" 6" 1' 3' 3'
6" 6" 6' 1' 1'6" 2'
6" 6" 6'

The top view featured is for the Alpha portion of the playground, shown at far left in the photo.

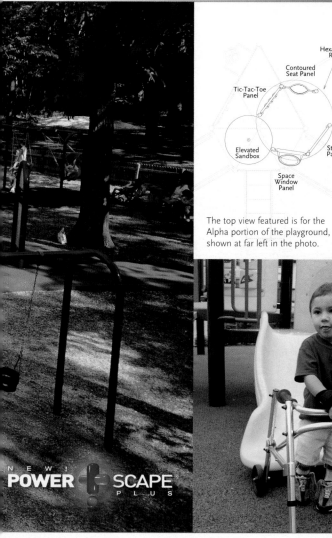

NEW!
POWER SCAPE PLUS

This playground in Maryland is another example of GameTime's dedication to integrated play for all Let us help you achieve your dream. Choose from our library of pre-designed accessible playgrounds, or let us create one to meet your specific needs.

PLAY FOR EVERYONE

All children deserve the opportunity to play. At GameTime, we can help you build a playground to make it possible.

PLAY WITH NO LIMITS

A leader in playground accessibility, GameTIme goes beyond access, making sure their products also allow integrated play opportunities for children of all abilities.

The first step to a fun play experience is access to the playground.

1-800-235-2440   WWW.GAMETIME.COM

Just because a child can access a play component, doesn't guarantee that it's fun. At GameTime, we create accessible play opportunities that kids want to return to again and again.

The second step is to make sure the play components are truly fun and enjoyable!

A PLAYCORE COMPANY
GameTime®
Enriching Childhood Through Play℠

GROUNDS
FOR
PLAY ℠
creative play environments

More than "accessible items"

Other companies see a child in a wheelchair and provide an elevated sandbox; Grounds For Play sees the emotional needs of the child and provides an integrated sand <u>experience</u>. While the elevated sandbox provides access to sand, the child needs access to **play! ...with his peers! ...in an *integrated* setting!**

Our corner chair is one small innovation that points out a big difference in our approach: Allowing children with special needs to be "one of the guys", not relegated to the fringes or to using only the "adaptive equipment".

1.800.552.PLAY • www.groundsforplay.com

integrating environments!

● We start with a "listening" approach, analyzing the site, interviewing the staff, teachers, or community leaders who will be working with children, and getting to know the children.

● Then we interactively design the play environment, taking into account over 40 factors that determine the direction of the design*.

● We provide accurately scaled site plans for the <u>whole</u> play environment (not just the equipment) and many site construction details are reviewed with the customer.

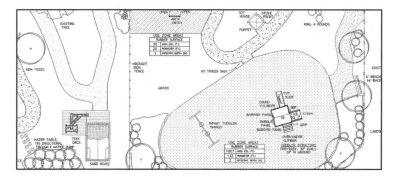

● **Unique** equipment can be custom designed and built, tailored to the site and to the particular IEP (Individual Educational Plan) in place for the children.

*Grounds For Play's design department can work closely with a customer's designer, such as Boundless Playgrounds, to provide technical assistance, product design, and project management services. Grounds For Play does not charge its clients for any consultation or design services. This applies whether the client works directly with Grounds For Play, or indirectly through a primary agreement with Boundless Playgrounds.

Grounds For Play provides "full-service" playground development, from design through site preparation, safety surfacing, landscaping and paved pathways. It is this fully integrated approach that makes truly integrating environments possible.

Look closely and you'll see the many details that create an **integrating playground experience.**

A key to creating an integrating play environment is the coordination of the various surfaces on the playground. Transitions from pathways to grass, from ramps to pathways, and from resilient surfaces to pathways, must be planned and executed to create both access and organization.

Extended Decks for front wheels of wheelchairs

A.

B.

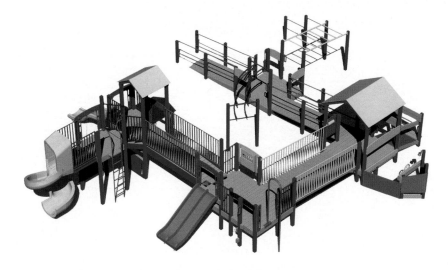

C.

D.

E.

The coordination of the various aspects of the process—from design to construction to final staff training—makes Grounds For Play your best source for playground development. We congratulate Boundless Playgrounds for their contribution to the country's children. We are proud to be a cooperating partner in their efforts.

GROUNDS FOR PLAY
creative play environments

1.800.552.PLAY • www.groundsforplay.com

A. Upper body slide   **B.** Proprioceptive Hammock.   **C.** Bowling Buddy   **D.** Texture Floor   **E.** Sand Bank.

MAKING CHILD'S PLAY WORK.

PROGRESS IN PROCESS

Developmentally speaking, play is kids' most important job. Whether they realize it or not, children are making all kinds of important progress as they're running, jumping, climbing, and interacting. That's why HAGS designs components that encourage development of gross and fine motor skills, intellect, and learning—not to mention the sheer fun of playing!

Research has shown that exercise helps kids learn more easily in all areas. For example, Howard Gardner's study of children in a Japanese pre-school showed that close supervision in small areas suppresses a child's independence and growth, whereas larger, better-equipped play areas encourage growth and initiative. Because children have no choice but to develop in the environment they're placed into, HAGS manufactures products that optimize that environment's potential.

670-103US

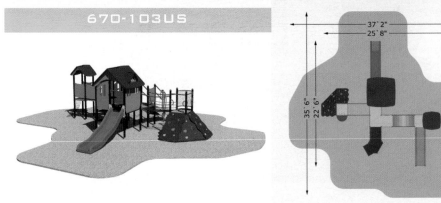

BETTER PRODUCTS. BETTER PLAY.

PLAY VALUE

HAGS' products make almost any play space a better environment for healthy, happy growth. Contact us for details on our complete line of play equipment for younger children, including these:

UniMini Play Structures
A uniquely European style, specially designed for early childhood. Choose from models like the Tignes, Lillehammer, Cortina, Albertville, and more!

Sand And Water Play
Together, sand and water create terrific learning opportunities—and natural fun! HAGS' offerings are simple, reliable, and accessible.

Spring Rockers
Smooth, comfortable double-milled edges and an enclosed rocking mechanism make these perennial favorites that kids simply love to ride.

HAGS PLAY USA

A Division Of PLAYPOWER, INC.

1-866-KIDS-PLAY (543-7752) • WWW.HAGS.COM

KOMPAN Unique Playgrounds

NOVA Southeastern University
Jim & Jan Moran Family Center Village - Mailman Segal Institute for Early Childhood Studies

Kompan Unique Playgrounds has always been a leader in the playground industry promoting and designing inclusive play environments. Playgrounds should allow children of all abilities to enjoy the lifelong benefits of outdoor play. The play environments that we create include spaces that challenge and develop motor skills, allow autonomous and parallel play, and provide room for exploring with courage and curiosity.

We've created many innovative and inclusive play environments for children of all abilities. The Family Center on the campus of NOVA Southeastern University is one such site. As you can see from our work with the EDSA Design Team and NOVA Southeastern University, creating a rich, accessible play environment is possible. Come explore the world of Kompan.

Playground C "Art Gallery"
Infant and Toddler Program

Playground B "Urban Village"
Baudhuin Preschool Program

Building "A"

Building "B"

Playground C "Country Village"
Preschool Program

Playground D "Beach Side"
Parent and Child Program

Playground C - "Country Village" contains a variety of play activities from the KOMPAN
...nts and Elements product lines. These and other products can be
...d at www.kompan.com.

...awing to the right is the Illustrative Layout Plan (All playgrounds and equipment are
...cessible.)

Project Data

Project Name: NOVA Southeastern University, Jim & Jan Moran Family Center Village, Mailman Segal Institute for Early Childhood Studies (http://www.nova.edu/msi)

Location: Fort Lauderdale, Florida, USA

Client: NOVA Southeastern University

Period of Construction: Master Plan Began 1999, Detail Design Began 2000, Construction Began September 2002 & Completed June 2003

Landscape Architecture: EDSA

Other consultants: Boundless Playgrounds (Playgrounds), Flynn Engineering (Civil), EDA (Lighting), Smallwood, Reynolds, Stewart, Stewart & Associates, Inc. (Architecture)

Playground Area: 17,000sf
Building Footprint Area: Building "A" 30,087sf
Building "B" 29,621sf - North Pavilion 900sf
South Pavilion 1,500sf

Site construction Specification: Kompan Playground Equipment, Color Rubber Surface, Concrete Path, Color Concrete Paving, Concrete Pavers, Concrete Wall with Stucco Finish, Architectural Styrofoam, Aluminum Gate and Fencing

About EDSA:

The EDSA Design Team is made up of (left to right) Rebecca Barber - Senior Design Staff, Joe Lallli - Managing Principal, Akiko Iwata - Senior Associate, Kona Gray - Vice President. EDSA has established itself as one of the leading planning, landscape architectural and graphic design firms in the world.   To learn more about EDSA you may visit their website at www.edsaplan.com.

About Jim and Jan Family Center Village:

NOVA Southeastern University is located in Fort Lauderdale, Florida and is one of the nation's top ten private nonprofit universities in the United States. The 300 acre NSU Campus Master Plan is a "Living Document" that responds to projected growth.

As the campus master plan architects, EDSA was challenged with providing a site for

Family Center within the NSU Master Plan in 1999.

The concept is based on a "village" of learning cottages which engages indoor and outdoor environments throughout the facility. The architecture protects outdoor areas between buildings making them ideal for playgrounds. Classrooms have been juxtaposed to outdoor play decks that serve as transition spaces to the adjacent playgrounds.

Kompan Play Consultants worked with EDSA to provide them with play equipment that would create a unique play environment that every child could enjoy. It was important to provide a variety of elements for interaction between specific age groups. Playground elements were placed appropriate distances from each other to create several smaller spaces within the playground resulting in a variety of choices for kids to play.

Rubber surfacing was utilized on the playgrounds. A variety of colors and patterns on the rubber surface psychologically defined the safety zones and circulation as well as articulating the theme of each playground.

Kompan playground equipment was selected based on several criteria such as educational purpose, safety, and maintenance issues.

The Family Center Village opened its doors in June 2003. When we all see the smiles of children and their parents at the Family Center

Village we understand the value of creating boundless playground and how Kompan proc can make every child enjoy the world of pla

Above & Left - Playground 'B' contains many products from the KOMPAN Elements line. These products include the Cottage (seen in the background of the left photo), Setting 1 (seen in the above photo on the left side), Spinner Bowl (seen in the forground of the left photo), and a Hopper (seen right side of the left photo). KOMPAN Elements are perfect for young children of all abilities in developing their motor skills, interacting with other children and learning more about the environment around them through experimentation. For more information on these and other Elements products, please visit www.kompan.com.

Cottage   Hopper   Spinner Bowl   Setting 1

The Infant Toddler Program, Playgrounds A and C, contain selections from the KOMPAN Moments product line. Featured here is the Moments Long Table above, to the right is the Fairy Castle, and obove right is the Mermaid's Fountain. All of these products are ADA accessible and provide many interesting and challenging activities. If you wish to find out more about these or other KOMPAN products, view our website at www.kompan.com.

Swing

Fairy Castle

MA Structure

Flowi

Navigator

Starfish

You and Me

Stinger

Mermaid's Fountain

Playground D - It is important to provide a variety of spaces and equipment for the interaction between age groups.

A combination of KOMPAN Moments and Elements structures is featured in the photos on this page. Both product lines offer a wide variety of activities for young children of all abilities.

In the above left photo is Playground 'A', which contains a Swing with infant seats, Little Daisy, Fairy Castle, a variety of tables and benches in different shapes and sizes, Daffodil, Daisy and a Tick Tock. All of these products provide a way for children to experiment with their surroundings.

In the middle left photo is Playground 'C' which features a KOMPAN Moments Structure, Blazer, Spinner Bowl, Rotating Sand Table, Workshop, Sand Slide, Mermaid's Fountain and a Starfish.

The photos below left and to the right show the KOMPAN Elements Flow 1 and Navigator, from Playground 'D'. This area also features a Stinger and a You and Me, both of which are toys that rock back and forth.

For more information on any of the KOMPAN Products shown here or other playground equipment, please contact KOMPAN Unique Playgrounds at:

KOMPAN
Unique Playgrounds
7717 New Market St.
Olympia, WA 98501
1.800.426.9788
www.kompan.com.

Accessible is good.
Inclusive is better.

Sway Fun™

An industry first: A wheelchair-accessible, totally inclusive glider that meets all safety standards. The only one of its kind, Sway Fun brings children with wheelchairs to the center of the action while enabling children of all abilities and adults to participate in a common activity. Sway Fun can accommodate up to 12 people, including two wheelchair passengers.

Thunderhead Climber™

Another innovation: The only climber in the industry that also functions as a transfer module. Thunderhead Climber is a multi-level structure offering children of all abilities a choice of three accessible climbing paths of varying difficulty to improve their physical confidence.

- Minimum area required: 53'x64'
- Total elevated components accessible by ramp: 16, required: 14
- Total elevated components accessible by transfer: 27, required: 0
- Total accessible ground level components: 1, required: 0

Landscape Structures takes an imaginative approach to designing barrier-free playgrounds by creating safe, stimulating, inclusive play environments that enable children of all ages and abilities to play together. These innovative designs combine wheelchair-accessible play equipment with free-standing structures to foster physical, cognitive and social development in all children.

Lava Run

This slide combines safe, boundless fun for toddlers and offers two creative options for imaginative, self-directed play: physical (slide features a safe entryway handlebar with extra-long exit area) and explorative (sculpted forms of plants and animals are found underneath).

Critter Canyon

This challenging climber boosts a child's imagination and offers a safe transfer point to a higher deck. Features sculpted forms of plants and animals that help make climbing easier and provides a visual and tactile sensation while playing.

Keys to Building Inclusive Playgrounds

• Design an accessible route of travel to the playground by installing the best surfacing material you can afford. Since it does little good to design fully accessible playstructures if children with disabilities can't get to the play area, think twice before using wood fiber or pea gravel and remember to install surfacing material that maximizes fall protection.

• Look at play from the point of view of children with disabilities, whether they are developmental, ambulatory, mental or visual. Do the right thing for them, and all kids will benefit.

• Require that the play equipment manufacturer indicate on the final plans all play events that are accessible, and to validate that the play area meets all current ADA Guidelines.

• Use only those play events that have been independently certified by the International Play Equipment Manufacturers Association (IPEMA).

• Include play events that enable children with disabilities to be at the center of the activity.

LANDSCAPE STRUCTURES INC

1.888.4FUNLSI   playlsi.com

More than just child's play.

Wheelchair-Accessible SuperScoop
This sturdy sand scooper is a great learning tool for little builders. Plus, it's designed for either standing play or easy, worry-free wheelchair access.

Learning Wall
LSI's approach to hands-on learning: A variety of panels placed at appropriate heights for accessibility provide individual skill builders for toddlers of all abilities.

Infant Maze
Designed specifically for younger children, these interactive activity panels are equipped with handles that support young children learning to stand and walk. Ground-level tunnels and panels help develop gross motor skills by providing lots of age-appropriate challenges.

Molded Bucket Seat Swings
The most popular swing design in the industry, the comfortable chair-like seat enables kids to play while providing a high, sturdy back for head, neck and back support.

For children ages one month to five years old, play habits are the building blocks for developing many vital, life-long skills. Children need the opportunity to make their own choices, to gain autonomy and master motor skills, make discoveries and experience consequences. As originators of play events, children choose their own preferred play path and learn the benefits of self-directed play.

A young child's determination to achieve independence is reflected in how they explore the world around them. By providing age-appropriate and developmental play equipment that challenges and inspires, children experience the incremental success they need to learn and grow.

CoolToppers™

The industry's first fully integrated shade systems, these high-density Shadesure® fabric roofs are a full-coverage solution to the shade requirement for early childhood centers. They block up to 90% of the sun's harmful UV rays and keep play areas up to 30°F cooler.

Chimes Panel

This inclusive panel incorporates musical play on the playground and is wheelchair accessible at the ground level.

Reach Panels

LSI's easy-to-reach Play Panels allow curious children of all abilities to enjoy hours of interactive fun.

Block Climber

A multi-level path allows kids to develop balance and spatial relationship skills as they step or climb from block to block. Available in a variety of fun and challenging configurations.

To learn more about independent play and inclusive play environments, contact:

LANDSCAPE STRUCTURES INC

1.888.4FUNLSI   playlsi.com

MAKE THE CHALLENGE MATCH THE CHILD.

There's a crucial disparity between the skills of younger children and their school-age counterparts. While preschoolers learn to interact, they're also gaining agility with lots of running, jumping, and climbing. Miracle can help you meet those vastly different developmental needs safely and effectively—starting with a huge selection of products designed for early childhood.

With Miracle, you'll find everything from toddler-sized play structures to balance beams to animated spring riders to climb-and-slide playpools. Each is designed to help younger kids build gross motor skills as they walk, climb, slide, and play together. Shown here is a small sampling of our extensive line of developmental Miracles. For more information on early childhood products, contact your exclusive Miracle Consultant or visit us on line: www.miracle-recreation.com.

MIRACLE.
RECREATION EQUIPMENT COMPANY

1-800-523-4202 · www.miracle-recreation.com

A Division Of PLAYPOWER, INC.

It may be smaller in stature, but Tots' Choice® includes the same high-quality materials and most of the components available in Miracle's larger playsystems. These little playsystems are a great fit for younger kids.

Smaller Deck Sizes
42" x 42" Square decks allow adequate play space for smaller budgets. Triangle and half-hexagon-shaped decks open up unique possibilities.

Shorter Deck Heights
Decks lower than 6' make playsystems more appropriate for younger children.

Exclusive Gripping Surfaces
Diamond-embossed and fluted gripping surfaces are specially designed for smaller hands.

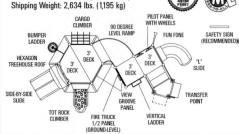

TOTS' CHOICE®　#718-073

Ground Space: 26' x 13' (8m x 4m)
Protective Area: 39' x 26' (11.9m x 8m)
Shipping Weight: 2,634 lbs. (1,195 kg)

This model is shown with loose-fill engineered wood fiber and Primary color combination.

This play area meets ADA guidelines for accessible components.

Miracle strongly suggests that a safety sign stating age-appropriateness and safety rules be displayed on every playground. An appropriate energy-absorbing surface is required under all play equipment.

WE HAVE A FEEL FOR FUN.

Toddlers' Choice™ allows even your littlest ones to experience safe, educational fun just like the "big" kids. Three models with molded-in shapes and animals, multiple deck heights, and exclusive components create the perfect environment for kids to learn and play together.

Miracle's sister company, Soft Play, helped pioneer "soft" playgrounds more than 18 years ago. One of their innovations is the Toddler Climb & Slide PlayPool. It provides a developmentally advantageous play activity for pre-schools and day-care centers, and is also great for restaurants, hotels, and retail stores.

Soft Shapes climbers and animals are lightweight, compact, and versatile—perfect for limited spaces. These squeezable, vinyl-covered foam play pieces offer long-lasting, interactive fun. And they're all designed to make the fun of hopping, rolling, and tumbling softer and safer.

Contact your exclusive Miracle Consultant for a free brochure.

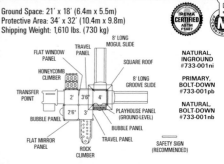

TODDLERS' CHOICE™ #733-001pi

Ground Space: 21' x 18' (6.4m x 5.5m)
Protective Area: 34' x 32' (10.4m x 9.8m)
Shipping Weight: 1,610 lbs. (730 kg)

NATURAL, INGROUND #733-001ni
PRIMARY, BOLT-DOWN #733-001pb
NATURAL, BOLT-DOWN #733-001nb

This inground model is shown with loose-fill engineered wood fiber and Primary color combination.

To meet ADA guidelines, this play area needs 2 additional accessible ground-level components (2 different activity types) which are not shown in the photo.

Miracle strongly suggests that a safety sign stating age-appropriateness and safety rules be displayed on every playground. An appropriate energy-absorbing surface is required under all play equipment.

Soft Shapes Corner Climber #441-2

· Six soft, interchangeable, tough-stitched pieces
· Fits neatly into almost any corner of a room
· Ideal for very young children
· Shapes can be assembled in seconds and can be moved around easily
· Hook-and-loop fasteners keep shapes in place

Floor Space: 5' x 5' (1.5m x 1.5m) Shipping Weight: 50 lbs. (23 kg)

Toddler Climb & Slide PlayPool #F12321-54

· Multiple activities for younger kids
· Spacious PlayPool stimulates imaginative play
· PlayPool includes hundreds of primary-colored balls
· Durable Rockite® (plastic) construction
· Includes Mira-Lene™ Panel with Wheel and Mirror

Floor Space: 8'8" x 5'8" x 6'4" (2.6m x 1.7m x 1.9m) Shipping Weight: 465 lbs. (211 kg)
The Toddler Climb and Slide PlayPool requires a 6' use zone employing impact-absorbing safety surfacing.

Therapeutic Sandbox #418-154

· Elevated cloverleaf design for children of all abilities
GS: 7' x 7' (2.1m x 2.1m) Weight: 450 lbs. (204 kg)

Paint Easel Panel #435

· See-through panel with erasable surface
GS: 2' x 5' (.6m x 1.5m) Weight: 100 lbs. (45 kg)

park
a PlayCore company
structures®
Maximizing the Potential of Play™

ABOUT THIS STRUCTURE

Size	31' x 45'
Use Zone	43' x 57'
Capacity	40 children

The **Park Structures playground** featured is a ramped structure that incorporates several different deck heights and difficulty levels that are play-useful for children of all abilities within the Basic and Transitional play phases. The ramped design allows all children to access even the vistas of the structure. Upon entering the structures from a ramp, steps, balancing activity or climbing component children have several choices of components on which to play either independently or inter- actively which in this play environment includes an abundance of complexity for young minds and bod- ies. Climbing options include ramps for full-body support , ladders for vertical challenge and stairs for upright climbing. These choices help to encourage self-directed play. Children can demonstrate parallel play on this structure when typically developing children and children with disabilities play together on the components. Parallel play is incorporated into this structure when a child is using the ADA Driving Panel and one is using the talk tube side by side. The abundance of play components on this structure allows this interactive play to take place. Inherent in the design of the structure is the encouragement for children to demonstrate looping within their predictable play behaviors. Looping on this structure may involve climbing the stairs to the deck, sliding down the curved slide and then repeating over and over again. While demonstrating looping, the child is gathering sen- sory experiences of both climbing and slid- ing. Overall, this structure designed for the Basic play phase of childhood incorporates several opportunities for interaction between typically developing children and children with disabilities, all within this play-useful sensory-stimu- lating design.

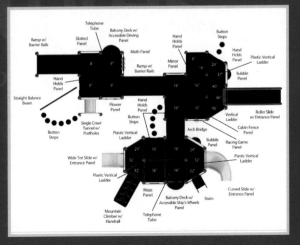

Mirror Panel

A mirror panel can often create a ground level or accessible deck-level cozy spot for use by children with mild, moderate and profound impairments.

park
a **PlayCore** company

structures®

Maximizing the Potential of Play™

Incorporating slight themes into this play structure attracts children to play while the dynamic play components hold their attention visit after visit to this Park Structures playground.

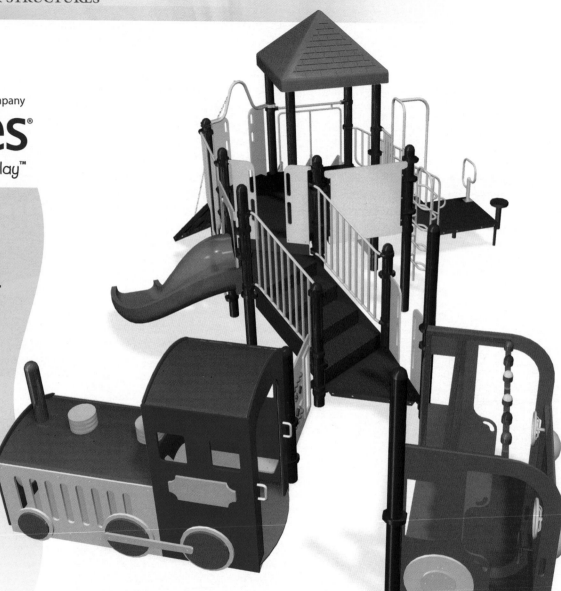

The unique themed components of this structure attract the

attention of children and create cozy spots that fully engage children in play, which sparks the developmental benefits to begin upon entering the structure. This structure incorporates four of these important cozy spots including those within the themed structures that are accessible at ground level. The four tight loops incorporate various climbers offering graduated levels of climbing for children at various stages of development. The transfer point allows for climbing with all four points of contact, the inclined Mountain Climber is an intermediate step before a child masters the Vertical Ring Climber. This structure packs a lot of play value in a small amount of space with a carrying capacity

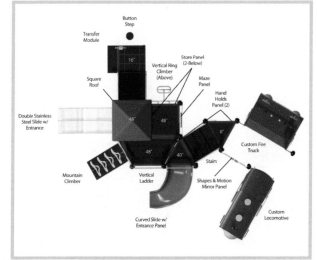

of 27 children engaged in play.

The unique and fresh equipment engross children who are in the early play phases. The manipulative activities incorporated in the locomotive and fire truck present an ever-changing environment to vary children's experiences each time they visit the play structure. Transfer accessibility and innovative ground level components allow children of all abilities to have access to this unique playground structure. The unique feature of the double-bedway stainless steel slide provides children with cochlear implants an exciting sliding experience without the fear of electro-static discharge erasing the mapping of the device. Incorporating slight themes into this play structure attracts children to play while the dynamic play components hold their attention visit after visit to this Park Structures playground.

Curved Slide

The Curved Slide allows children of all abilities to experience the sensory sensation of sliding.

ABOUT THIS STRUCTURE	
Size	27' x 23'
Use Zone	39' x 35'
Capacity	27 children

2+2 Swinger

The movement provided by the 2+2 Swinger provides pleasurable sensory experience for children. The spring rider can be used by two or four children playing simultaneously. A large, flat foot rest panel and seats with low back supports provide a feeling of security for the riders. When accommodating four children, two of the participants assume the more challenging standing position.

Crawl Tunnel

Connecting platforms with Crawl Tunnels on a play structure encourages children to change their body position as they travel from one area of the play system to another. Children can experience the structure in a creeping posture as well as an erect walking posture.

Table and Seat for Two

The Table and Seat for Two creates a cozy spot in the under-deck area where children in the transitional play phase can gather, compare arrange and sort items that they collect around the playground.

park
a **PlayCore** company
structures®
Maximizing the Potential of Play™

Music Panel

The Park Structures music panel is a manipulative component which also provides auditory sensory stimulation for children.

Spin & Win Panel

The Spin & Win Panel, exclusively designed by Park Structures, encourages positive competition and interaction between children. The panel is specifically designed to accommodate children using mobility devices so they can be an integral part of the fun.

This Structure provides cozy spots for children underneath decks at ground level.

This Structure contains

- Lilly Pad climber and Steps
- ADA Transfer Station
- Zig Zag Balance Beam
- Bedrock Climber
- Set of Talk Tubes
- 90° Curve Slide
- Gated Rung Ladder
- Bubble panel
- Square Ridge Roofs
- Store Front Panel

- Gear Panel
- Pipe Wall
- Pipe wall with Wheel
- Inclined Crawl Tunnel
- Triple Rail Slide
- Educational Climber
- Cargo Net Climber
- Clover Climber
- Window Panel with Seat
- Store Front Panel

Building Tomorrows Play Environments Today

This Playland Play structure allows children to play in a looping pattern from lily pad steps to balance beam.

Safe use Zone
45' X 29'
13.7 X 8.8 m

This Playland Component provides platforms of different heights and shapes for opportunities to climb or use cross-lateral movement.

PLAY LAND

Building Tomorrows Play Environments Today

Contact Person:
Richard Holbrook
800 356 4727
richardh@playland-inc.com

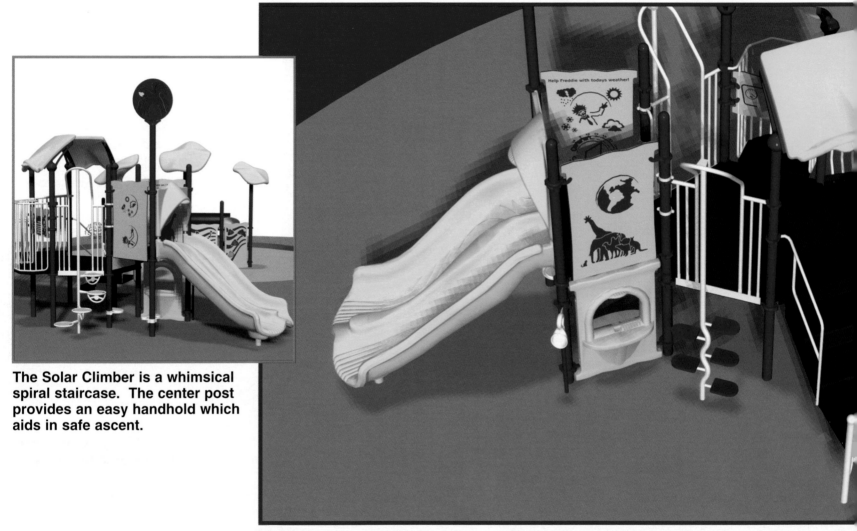

The Solar Climber is a whimsical spiral staircase. The center post provides an easy handhold which aids in safe ascent.

Help Freddie with todays weather!

The Beanstalk Climber and Transfer Station provide routes of differing challenge to reach

When trust matters.

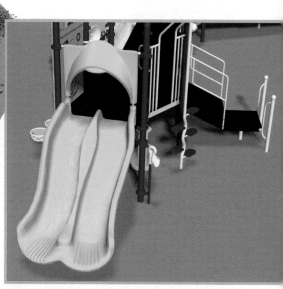

the slide.

The
Storefront
Panel makes
use of under-deck
space and encourages
social interaction.

The Twist and Shout Double Glide
Slide gives two different experiences,
with curved and textured bedways.
It can be reached by four different
climbers, plus the wheelchair ramp.

Colors, sounds, moving parts, cozy spaces, climbers and slides all combine to provide activities for all children to play independently or together.

A whole section of bells, chimes and drums encourages children to express themselves with sound and activity. The drums and the bell half panel allow children in wheelchairs to join the fun.

The Driver Panel allows children to explore the effect of spinning knobs and race track fun. Helps develop manual dexterity and a healthy attitude about competition.

The Accessible Solar Half Panel not only adds visual appeal, but also incorporates additional play value to the structure. Half Panels allow activity for all children including children in wheelchairs.

Multiple loops offer a variety of activities, with climbing, crawling, sliding and balancing options for children at all levels of ability.

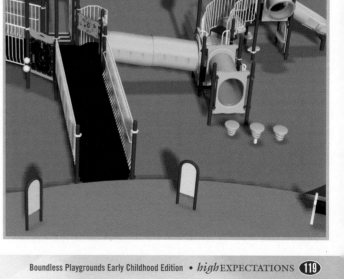

PLAYWORLD SYSTEMS®

When trust matters.

The ToddlerTown™ Village provides little ones with cozy spaces and crawl tubes, and even includes an art panel for children to show their artistic ability. Talking Bob is a kid-powered interactive audible experience ideal for all ability levels.

Crawl Tubes and Bounce Buttons create an inviting loop with a deck or a wheelchair ramp, and a Babble-On talk tube encourages children to verbally express themselves.

Bernie Bus is spring mounted, with dual steering wheels, rattle knobs and an accessible entrance.

PLAYWORLD SYSTEMS®
When trust matters.

1000 Buffalo Road
Lewisburg, PA 17837-9795 U.S.A.
Phone: (570) 522-9800 Toll-Free: 800-233-8404 Fax: (570) 522-3030
www.playworldsystems.com

The Deep Rung Arch Climber is ergonomically designed for safe ascent and easy step-off. The graduated rung depths keep children upright throughout the climb. The Sonic Slide is a super winding ride with high sides which reduces the risk of falls. The Sonic Slide is segmented allowing flexibility in design.

Transition platforms help youngsters with disabilities access play activities.

Many structures also feature wheelchair ramps.

Li'L Climber Available with RCI's earth-friendly PlasTECH™ uprights or recycled steel with long lasting powder coat finish. Two different sliding experiences with a loop climber entrance. Transition platform allows children with physical challenges to access the Li'l Climber play center. Weighs 1,471 lbs.
15' x 16' ground space, 27' x 29' use zone.

RECREATION CREATIONS inc.

Transition Platform with Hand Rail

Heritage Roof Shades Large Deck

"L" Tube Slide

Extra Wide Slide

Loop Arch Climber

Tugboat Lots of ground-level play activities. Porthole bubble panels, double wide slide, chain net climber, pipe wall with captain's wheel, large deck with transition platform. Uprights are RCI patented steel reinforced recycled PlasTECH™.
Weighs 2,786 lbs. Needs 19' x 28' ground space with 33' x 40' use zone.

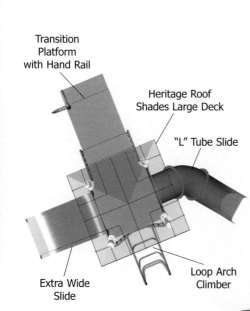

Baby Stegosaurus
A climber with personality! Textured powder coat finish on galvanized recycled steel has the look and feel of dinosaur skin. Stands only 4' high so even very small children climb with ease. Weighs 259 lbs. Requires 6' x 13' ground space with 18' x 25' use zone.

Lochie Sea Serpent Climber
This fun-loving three section Serpent has plenty of climbing and crawling activities. Panels are high density polyethylene with deep etched graphics. Head stands 44" high, center is 24" and tail 37". Weighs 53 lbs. Allow 9'6" x 21'6" use zone when all sections are positioned.

Magic Frog Sandbox
Features four seats and four tables for sand play activities. Frog graphic is cut into high density polyethylene. 95" square, 27" high. Weighs 241 lbs.

Wiggle Buddies
Zebb Zebra and our bright yellow Wonder Bus are set on coated tempered steel coil springs and feature a foot support, handhold and seat with back for safety and comfort. Side panels are tri-mold polyethylene, with permanent etched graphics. Panels will last a lifetime and never need to be painted. Weighs 58 lbs. 12' x 12' minimum use zone.

Tiny Tot Table Made of high density polyethylene guaranteed to last a lifetime! Oval top with rounded attached seats. 44" x 39½" x 19" high. Weighs 65 lbs.

Puppet Theatre Play Panel Stage graphic is routed into two-color polyethylene panel. Mount between free standing posts or on a larger play structure. 39" x 42" panel weighs 57 lbs.

Giraffe Bench Complete your playground with a comfortable place to rest. Whimsical polyethylene end-panels never need painting! A full 73" long and 37" high. Weighs 122 lbs.

Talk Tube Talk and listen to friends on the other side of the play structure. Powder coated steel. Pair of tubes 45 lbs.

RECREATION
CREATIONS inc.

toward safe INCLUSIVE PLAY

toward safe INCLUSIVE PLAY

Authors' Note: The National Center for Boundless Playgrounds has a longstanding relationship with many organizations that promote playground safety. This chapter, written by our associates at the National Program for Playground Safety (NPPS), has been included to bring attention to their work as the nation's leading organization solely focused on playground safety. The staff at NPPS collaborates with the U.S. Consumer Product Safety Commission and the American Society for Testing and Materials to raise public awareness offer the need to remove the causes of child injuries on public playgrounds. Within this chapter the four major playground injury risk factors are identified and solutions are recommended. These recommendations are based on current "best practices" and are the opinions of Dr. Donna Thompson, and Dr. Susan Hudson, and Heather Olsen, the authors of this chapter. All of the benefits to children that can be achieved during engaged play would be lost if these exciting play environments weren't also SAFE.

T HE MISSION OF THE NATIONAL PROGRAM FOR Playground Safety is to raise awareness about the need for playground safety and injury prevention at the national, state, and local levels. In that regard, the program addresses four risk factors:

- The need for adult supervision of children on the playground.

- The need for children to be directed to appropriate developmentally designed playground environments, either designed for ages 2-5 or 5-12.

- The need for appropriate fall surfacing of sand, pea gravel, wood products, and rubber products—never asphalt, cement, dirt or grass.

- The need for equipment and surfacing maintenance to maintain the depth of the surfacing and to prevent spaces between three and a half inches and nine inches where children might strangle.

The program encourages adults to continue their efforts to provide safe equipment and environmental conditions on playgrounds so that children can do what they do best: play! The National Program for Playground Safety is funded by the Centers for Disease Control and Prevention and is located at the University of Northern Iowa, Cedar Falls, Iowa 50614-0618.

For more information or materials about SAFE: call 1.800.554.7529 or visit www.uni.edu/playground.

we can have SAFE PLAYGROUNDS!

AS HAS BEEN DOCUMENTED THROUGHOUT THE CHAPTERS of *High Expectations*, play is essential to the development of all children. Chapter 3 details the predictable play behaviors of children. Chapter 5 discusses the need for keeping the play experience fresh, and Chapter 7 touches on the site details that enhance the play experience. The final key to these play experiences is that they should occur without the fears and tears found in many play environments.

Jeremy is a bright and energetic four-year-old who loves to run and climb with his fellow preschoolers. The fact that he has a slight limp and weakness in his right arm as the result of a mild case of cerebral palsy does not usually slow him down. On this particular day, his class of 20 had gone to the park to play on the large playground's play structures. As it occurred, when the class got to the edge of the play area, the teacher and her aide let the children dash off to the structure to play. Some of the children ran up the structure and across a long ramp to slide down an eight-foot-high curved slide. Others chose to climb up that curved slide from the bottom. Meantime, Jeremy decided to explore a structure that challenged his climbing abilities. Somehow, he managed to struggle to the top. As he reached for the deck, he slipped and caught himself by his hands. Hanging from the deck, he screamed for help. Fortunately, another adult who was visiting the playground rescued Jeremy from an unnecessary fall.

The question is how could this incident have been avoided?

The NPPS addresses the playground environment in terms of four injury risk factors—**S**upervision, **A**ppropriate developmental design, **F**all surfacing, and **E**quipment and surfacing maintenance. The first letters of these areas form the acronym **SAFE**, the kind of playground that you should expect for your children. Not paying attention to these four areas can raise the possibility that an injury might occur.

Risk is defined as the probability of loss or injury. When your doctor informs you that you are at risk for a heart attack, she is basing that prognosis on the fact that you have high blood pressure, high cholesterol, a family history of heart disease, or a combination of those factors. The more risk factors present, the higher the probability of a heart attack. Taken in the same light, the more playground injury risk factors present, the greater likelihood that a child will be injured. Let's reflect on Jeremy's situation to see how these SAFE risk factors interacted to create an unsafe play environment.

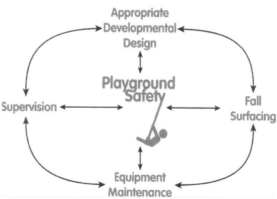

s is for SUPERVISION

THE FIRST THING THAT MUST BE UNDERSTOOD IS THAT equipment does not supervise children, only adults do. Good supervision is more than just watching. It is the active, yet unobtrusive, monitoring of the environment to keep children safe from hazards and to promote injury prevention. Part of good supervision is directing children to play on equipment that is appropriate for their developmental ability. In Jeremy's case, the supervisor took the children from the preschool to a playground that was designed for children ages 2-12. The problem in this instance is that the play equipment that was designed specifically for ages 2-5 was linked by a ramp to the equipment that was designed for ages 5-12. As a result, the supervisors allowed Jeremy and other preschoolers to be, at risk by letting them explore all of the equipment. They should have checked the area ahead of playtime to learn which areas were appropriate for preschoolers. Although the equipment for ages 2-5 was lower, no signage or labeling informed adults where the separation occurred.

What could the supervisors have done to prevent Jeremy's plight and given him a more appropriate challenge? They could have:

1. Visited the playground to decide where preschool children should play.

2. Designated an adult to stand between the 2-5 and 5-12-year-old equipment to prevent Jeremy and the other preschoolers from using equipment that was not developmentally appropriate for them. An ounce of prevention could have prevented an accident and minutes of agony.

In addition, if age-appropriate signage had been posted outside the area and age-appropriate labeling had been located on the equipment, the supervising adults would have directed the children to the suitable equipment, and Jeremy could have enjoyed a fun, challenging outing rather than facing the risk of an injury.

a is for appropriate DEVELOPMENTAL DESIGN

WHAT ABOUT APPROPRIATE DEVELOPMENTAL DESIGN? Although the equipment on the playground followed the conventional wisdom of designing for children ages 2-12, Jeremy did not know that. He liked to climb, so he headed for a place to challenge his interests. Unfortunately, the ladder was designed for children ages 5-12. The distances between the steps were a huge struggle. He was fortunate that he did not fall while reaching for each step. Then, he tried to reach across to the deck, missed his footing and caught the deck with his hands. The fall to the surface from his handhold was six feet. His crying could be heard all over the park. Before intervention, he was at risk for the possibility of a broken arm or concussion.

How could this risk have been avoided?

1. Adults needed to know which equipment was designed for ages 2-5 and which for ages 5-12. In addition, the equipment should have been physically separated.

2. Because the equipment was not physically separated, the adults needed to decide which equipment was appropriate for the developmental abilities of the children for whom they were responsible.

Unfortunately, this playground only provided three items that safely suited these children's developmental needs—a ramp, a lower slide and a manipulative play panel. Supervisors need to understand that one size does not fit all. In this particular case, it might have meant a decision to go to another playground where more suitable play environment choices were available for children ages 2-5.

f is for FALL SURFACING

NOW, LET'S LOOK AT THE PLAY ENVIRONMENT SURFACING. In this situation, the playground was covered with pea gravel. While pea gravel is one of the four suitable loose-fill surfaces noted earlier, at a depth of nine inches, it only provides adequate shock absorption (impact attenuation) for falls to

the surface up to five feet in height, no matter the depth of the pea gravel. The NPPS recommends 12 inches of loose fill surfacing, no matter the type selected, because regular maintenance rarely keeps the depth of the surface to its recommended depth. In this case, the use zone only had six inches of pea gravel. (The use zone is the area under and around equipment where it is expected that a child might fall. For stationary equipment, the use zone extends six feet in all directions.) NPPS also recommends that wood products (wood chips or engineered wood fibers), sand, rubber mats, or poured-in-place products are more suitable surfaces for play areas designed for preschoolers. The latter two are easier to maintain and provide an even surface on which children can crawl or walk. Thus, Jeremy and the other children were placed at risk because the surface would not adequately cushion a fall.

Other negatives about pea gravel are that it is not recommended for preschoolers, as it may become part of their diet and, by its very nature, it does not allow children who use wheelchairs or other mobility aids to get to the equipment. Thus, unless an accessible path that was firm, stable, and slip-resistant was provided elsewhere to the playground equipment from a parking area, the playground wasn't suitable for any of Jeremy's classmates who have mobility impairments. This park playground is noncompliant with the ADAAG Final Rule for Play Areas and all the tenets of inclusive play that have been covered in *High Expectations*.

What should the supervisors have done? They should have:

1. Explored the playground to determine the suitability of the surfacing.

2. Taken the children to another site that had appropriate surfacing for preschoolers.

In addition, the park department should be encouraged to install a surfacing that is more appropriate for the use zone and targeted ages of the children.

e is for equipment
AND SURFACING MAINTENANCE

THE FINAL RISK FACTOR THAT PLAYED A PART IN THE potential injury to Jeremy involved equipment and surfacing maintenance. Upon inspection, no problems were found with the equipment. This was not the case, however, with the condition of the surfacing. If the supervisors had inspected the area, they would have realized that:

1. Pea gravel was an inappropriate surface for preschoolers.

2. The pea gravel depth was not proportionate to the height of the equipment, even for school-age children.

What should the supervisors have done?

They should have eliminated the risk to their charges by taking them to a play area that had appropriate surfacing and sufficient depth of surfacing even for school-age children.

toward safer INCLUSIVE PLAY

AS WE HAVE DEMONSTRATED, THE SAFE MODEL IS interactive, that is, no one risk factor is more important than the others. Rather, as illustrated in this case, by changing the surfacing of the playground in question, the risk factor would only be reduced by one quarter – in other words one factor of four. What caring adults need to consider is the total play environment and how all four of these elements interact to produce safe play areas.

High Expectations has outlined the fundamental principles of creating inclusive play experiences for children of all abilities. By following those principles within the SAFE framework, play environments can, indeed, be produced that safely meet the needs of all children and reduce safety risks. ❖

glossary

T O CLEARLY EXPRESS THE IDEAS OUTLINED IN *High Expectations*, the authors and the National Center for Boundless Playgrounds developed a new set of terms to compliment commonly used industry terms. Each of the terms has been defined and correlated to the Play Behavior Framework. The larger triangle on the graphic next to each definition indicates the segment of Play Behavior Framework it is related to (Play Behavior Phases, Play Environment Design Criteria, or Play Attraction Continuum). Also included are words, phrases and organizations that are not directly related to the National Center for Boundless Playgrounds or the Play Behavior Framework but are used within the playground industry. (These terms don't have a graphic next to them.)

Access Board, *n* - The Architectural and Transportation Barriers Compliance Board (Access Board) is an independent Federal agency devoted to accessibility for people with disabilities. To contact the Access Board - 1331 F Street, NW., suite 1000, Washington, DC 20004-1111.

Alpha Play Environment Grouping, *n* - the arrangement of play components and features designed to foster and support the predictable play behaviors of children in the basic and transitional play phases so that *all* children can achieve engaged play.

American Society for Testing and Materials (ASTM), *n* - Organized in 1998, ASTM Intl. is a not-for-profit organization that provides a forum for the development and publication of voluntary consensus standards for materials, products, systems, and services. To contact ASTM – 100 Barr Harbor Dr., West Conshohocken, PA 19428-2959 – (610) 832-9585 - www.astm.org

Americans with Disabilities Act Accessibility Guidelines (ADAAG), *n* – a document issued in 1991 by the Architectural and Transportation Barriers Compliance Board (Access Board) that contains general scoping and technical provisions that apply to all types of facilities. To receive a copy of the final rule for play areas contact the Access Board - Automated publications order line (202) 272-5434 or www.access-board.gov/play/finalrule.htm

GLOSSARY

Architectural Barrier, *n* – any structure or surface material that limits, restricts, or bars entrance. An architectural barrier is any abrupt change in elevation along a hard surface path of travel like a step, any surface like uneven grass or sand that cannot be crossed independently by a person using a wheelchair, or a curb that contains loose materials.

Autonomous Play, *n* – the term applied to independent, self-directed activity of children that is characterized by being alone; the preferred play type of the least play-sophisticated (typically youngest) children.

Basic Play Phase, *n* – the first division within childhood when the child is primarily motivated to collect and organize information that is physical and sensorial as demonstrated with activities that are repetitive in nature and by playing alone during an engaged play episode.

Beta Play Environment Grouping, *n* - the arrangement of play components and features designed to foster and support the predictable play behaviors of children in the transitional and complex play phases so that *all* children can achieve engaged play.

Branching, *v* – a more sophisticated play behavior than looping that couples movement and sensory experiences with child-initiated gathering of loose parts to

expand play in play episodes under the child's direction.

Circuit, *n* – a pattern support for motor skill looping on a composite play structure. A circuit is a series of play component parts in immediate proximity so that the user playing in a looping play behavior can see the beginning of the circuit from the ending point.

Complex Play Phase, *n* - the third division within the childhood play continuum when the child is primarily motivated to collect and organize information ethically as demonstrated by activities that are centered on rule-making and by assessing the fairness of ever-changing play circumstances with other children during an engaged play episode.

Complexity, *n* – the name given to any combination of features within a play environment, such as intersections, that supply children with abundant opportunities to make choices, and consequently, decisions they can use to discover the connections between concrete object and concepts.

Composite Play Structure, *n* – two or more play components (like slides, climbers, tunnels, bridges, play decks, balancing pods, or play panels) attached or directly adjacent, to create one integral unit that supports more than one play activity.

Cross Lateral Pattern, *n* - a sophisticated gross motor coordination skill typically mastered by a child during early childhood, demonstrated by climbing stairs or other play-structure climbing components that require alternating foot patterns, i.e., placing *only* one foot at each level of ascent or descent.

 Delta Play Environment Grouping, *n* - the arrangement of play components and features designed to foster and support the predictable play behaviors of children in the interdependent play phase and beyond, so that *all* children can achieve engaged play.

Design System, *n* – a method to replicate play-useful arrangements of play equipment and/or environmental features that are based upon the predictable play behaviors of children so that play choices are available to sustain them in each engaged play episode.

Developmental Advantage, *n* – the name for an active process where *all* children are allowed to unfold, gradually and in detail, the connections and relationships between concrete objects and concepts to form understandings; a favorable circumstance for child-directed discovery; providing the resources that support engaged play.

 Developmental Sequence, *n* - a series of changes in children from simple to more advanced physical, intellectual, ethical, and social abilities that promote adaptation to the environment and increased acceptance and participation in society.

Developmentally Appropriate, *adj.* – as this term applies to play environments, it describes meeting the particular developmental needs of the group for whom it is planned, matching current ability to activity.

Domain, *n* - a system to study human behavior; an organizational method used by adults, based on observation and categorization, to simplify the understanding of human development. In the study of play behavior, the recognition of a domain is based on the actions of children as they assign value and preference to similarly grouped play activities used during engaged play episodes.

Egocentric, *adj.* – the child's intrinsic concern and active drive to focus on their own activities and needs - a natural course that leads a child to the self-construction of their reality. The use of egocentric behaviors supports each child's discovery across the physical/sensory domain, the intellectual domain, the ethical domain, and the social domain.

Engaged Play, *n* – the compelling activity of children that both attracts and holds their attention; the characteristics of engaged play are eager willingness to participate, physically located at the core of activity, and primary initiator of the play event where children direct the outcome of the event.

Gamma Play Environment Grouping, *n* - the arrangement of play components and features designed to foster and support the predictable play behaviors of children in the transitional and complex play phases so that *all* children can achieve engaged play.

Impact-Attenuating Surfacing Material, *n* – any material that reduces or dissipates the energy of a falling body. These materials can be unitary (like manufactured rubber tile or pour-in-place surface), organic natural materials (like engineered wood fiber or wood chips) or inorganic materials (like sand, pea gravel or rice stone).

Intellectual Domain, *n* – the non-discrete organizational segment of human development that frames how children master the information they collect through the manipulation of concrete objects and apply it to the relationship of abstract concepts.

Interdependent Play Phase, *n* - the fourth division within the childhood play continuum when the child is primarily motivated to collect and organize information socially as demonstrated in child-directed group activities organized to either be collaborative or competitive during engaged play episodes.

Loop(ing), *n* - a repetitive play behavior that couples moving and gathering sensory experiences into play episodes under the child's direction.

Marking-Time Pattern, *n* – an immature gross motor movement used by a child during early childhood, demonstrated by climbing stairs or other play-structure climbing components using the same foot to lead (and the same foot to trail) at each level of ascent or descent.

Motor Planning, *n* – the process of mentally organizing a novel action; a cognitive process that precedes observable motor performance; involves the organization and timing and sequencing of actions. (Parham & Fazio, 1997, p251)

National Program for Playground Safety (NPPS), *n* – the nation's leading organization solely focused on playground safety. To contact NPPS at University of Northern Iowa, Cedar Falls, Iowa 50614-0618, 1-800-554-7529 or www.uni.edu/playground

National Recreation and Parks Association (NRPA), *n* – an organization whose mission is to advance parks, recreation, and environmental conservation efforts that enhance the quality of life for all people. This is the organization that sponsors the National Playground Safety Institute (NPSI) that provides training and testing to endorse Certified

Playground Safety Inspectors (CPSI). To contact NRPA for a CPSI in your area - 22377 Belmont Ridge Road Ashburn, VA 20148-4501 - (703) 858-0784 or www.nrpa.org

Neurological Development, *n* - a system of increased functional sophistication characterized by differentiation and integration. Differentiation is the process by which structure, function, or forms of behavior become more specialized. Integration refers to the intricate interweaving of neural mechanisms into a coordinated interaction (Gabbard, 1992, p6).

Neurological Pathways, *n* - pathways in the central nervous system consisting of neurons that receive, interpret, and alter information received from environmental input.

Nov'lication, *n* – a term that indicates variable characteristics that can be changed in a play setting according to a plan to introduce additional stimuli to children during play; an opportunity to attract a child's attention to enhance the productivity of play episodes.

Parallel Play, *n* – as part of a self-directed play episode, the child plays autonomously, but next to another child. The child's actions may mirror the actions of others with similar objects.

Pattern Support, *n* – the design system used for an ALPHA PEG layout; a sequence of play activities arranged to foster and support looping and branching play behaviors.

Physical - Social Domain, *n* – the non-discrete organizational segment of human development that frames how children master the information they collect through movement and sensation.

Play Attraction Continuum, *n* – a system of play facilitation based on predictable play behavior that provides children with developmental advantage by frequent changes to the play setting and the provision of progressively appropriate play materials.

Play Behavior Framework, *n* – an organizational method to focus on the details of how play environments are designed and facilitated to provide developmental advantage for *all* children.

Play Behavior Phases, *n* – a system of organizing multiple observable characteristics of children that supports the design and facilitation of play environments to achieve developmental advantage.

Play Behaviors, *n* - any behavior exhibited by the child reflecting a sense of intrinsic motivation, control, and enjoyment, to collect information about the locomotion, surrounding environment, social appropriateness, and the concept of self.

Play Environment Design Criteria, *n* – a system of play environment design based on predictable play behavior that provides children with developmental advantage by ensuring that the play setting is sufficiently complex to supply them with diverse explorations during multiple play episodes.

Play Environment Grouping (PEG), *n* – an arrangement of play components and features that are developmentally appropriate, rigorous and challenging; a place where engaged play occurs.

Play Usefulness, *n* – a term that describes the quality of suitability to support the independent, self-directed explorations of all children, with and without disabilities. The thoughtful combination of characteristics within play environments, playground designs, or playground elements that are developmentally advantageous and architecturally barrier-free for children of all abilities.

Preeminent Role, *n* - refers to the information collection and organizational preference of the child demonstrated during engaged play and associated with developmental domains.

Rigorous, *adj.* – used as a means to assess play value. During physical play activity, a change in energy expenditure, in workload, in mobility requirement, or in motor planning. During a play episode that is mainly a cognitive play activity, a change in demand for use of a cognitive strategy. In ethical play activity, a change in dissonance between right and wrong. In social play activities, a change in the requirements for working together in harmonious and productive groupings. During emotional arousal, a change in the requirement to assess, control, and use feelings to understand the meaning of information.

Sensory Integration, *n* - the ability of the brain to receive and organize sensory information allowing the individual to adapt to changes in the environment and participate in functional activities.

Socially Inviting, *adj.* - as this term applies to playgrounds, a public environment supportive of interpersonal relationships that is designed to provide developmental advantage, where *every child* experiences both the provision of accommodation and attitudes of mutual respect and acceptance that stimulates the development of each individual.

Stuff, *n* –the natural material like grass, pine needles, nuts, leaves, moss, stones, pinecones, berries, or sticks that children appropriate for engaged play episodes. Any of these materials can be specially assigned a role during play, or they can be used for experiments of the child's design.

Transitional Play Phase, *n* - the second division within the childhood play continuum when the child is primarily motivated to collect and organize information intellectually, as demonstrated by the manipulation and selective addition of loose parts, and by playing in parallel with other children during an engaged play episode.

Unitary Synthetic Material, *n* – a manufactured material used to provide an impact-attenuating surface. These materials can be rubber tiles, mats or a combination of rubber-like materials held together by a binder that may be poured in place at a playground site and cures to form a unitary shock-absorbing surface.

U.S. Consumer Product Safety Commission (USCPSC), *n* – an independent federal regulatory agency. The USCPSC works to save lives and keep families safe by reducing the risk of injuries and deaths associated with consumer products. The USCPSC provides "The Handbook for Public Playground Safety", at no charge. A copy of the handbook can be obtained by calling the USCPSC at (800) 638-2772.

suggested READING LIST

Damasio, A. R. *Descartes Error: Emotion, Reason and the Human Brain.* Quill, An Imprint of Harper Collins Publishers. 2000 (1994). ISBN# 0380726475

Frost, J. L. *Play and Playscapes.* Delmar Publishers Inc. 1992. ISBN# 0-8273-4699-9

Gibson, J.J. *The Ecological Approach to Visual Perception.* Houghton, Mifflin. 1979. ISBN# 0898599598

Ginsburg, H.P. & Opper, S. *Piaget's Theory of Intellectual Development.* Prentice Hall. 1988 (1969, 1979). ISBN# 0-13-675158-X

Hannaford, C. *Smart Moves, Why Learning Is Not All In Your Head.* Great Ocean Publishers. 1995. ISBN# 0-91556-27-8

Kamii, C. & DeVries, R. *Physical Knowledge in Preschool Education - Implications of Piaget's Theory.* Teachers College Press. 1993. ISBN# 0-8077-3254-0

Kutska, K. S., Hoffman, K. J. & Malkusak, A. C. *Playground Safety is No Accident, 3rd Edition.* National Recreation and Park Association. 2002. ISBN# 0-929581-32-6

McGraw, M.B. *The Neuromuscular Maturation of the Human Infant.* Hafner Publishing Company. 1963 (1945).

Montessori, M. *The Secret of Childhood.* Ballantine Books. 1981 (1972). ISBN# 0-345-30583-3

Montessori, M. *The Absorbent Mind.* Kalakshetra Publications. 1967. ISBN# 0805041567

Moore, R. C. *Plants for Play - A Plant Selection Guide for Children's Outdoor Environments.* MIG Communications. 1993. ISBN# 0-944661-18-1

Moore, R. C., Goltsman, S. M. & Iacofano, D. S. *Play for All Guidelines, 2nd Edition.* MIG Communications. 1992. ISBN# 0-944661-17-3

Piaget, J. *The Origins of Intelligence in Children.* International University Press. 1952. ISBN# 0823639002

Piaget, J. *The Child's Conception of the World.* Routledge and Kegan Paul, Ltd. 1951

Piaget, J. & Inhelder, B. *The Psychology of The Child.* Basic Books, Inc. 2000 (1969). ISBN# 0-465-09500-3

Piaget, J. & Inhelder, B. *The Child's Conception of Space.* The Norton Library, W.W. Norton & Company, Inc. 1967. ISBN# 0415168899

Rivkin, M. S. *The Great Outdoors - Restoring Children's Right To Play Outside.* National Association for the Education of Young Children. 1995. ISBN# 0-935989-71-4

Theemes, T. *Let's Go Outside - Designing the Early Childhood Playground.* High/Scope Press. 1999. ISBN# 1-57379-082-6

Wadsworth, B.J. *Piaget's Theory of Cognitive and Affective Development: Foundations of Constructivism (5th).* Longman Publishers. 1996. ISBN# 0801307732

DYNAMO

Techno Dynamo's products are made from the finest material available. Stainless steel, aluminum and galvanized steel are appropriately prepared and finished with vibrant polyester powder coating paint and plastisol PVC coatings. Techno Dynamo offers a conditional over all guaranty of one year from the date of purchase on all parts of the play equipment.

(800) 790-0034
www.sympatico.ca

MEYER DESIGN

- Play equipment in steel, wood, or recycled plastic lumber
- Innovative designs that work within your space requirements
- Wide range of color options with recycled plastic and steel
- Choices in play surfacing: wood fiber, poured-in-place rubber, etc.

(800) 543-9176
www.meyerdesign.com

SOFSURFACES INC.

When SofTILE Locks, it stays locked. Recent design improvements include our hollow-core stanchion which has increased the density of our tile while simultaneously increasing fall height protection. Higher density, better fall height ratings and the same great locking features are backed by an industry leading 5 year warranty for fall height performance.

(800) 263-2363
www.sofsurfaces.com

SOUND PLAY, INC.

Children everywhere celebrate their joys, lament their sorrows and express their love through the arts. To help fill this universal expressive need, Sound Play designs and builds tuned, weather resistant and durable outdoor musical instruments that provide an opportunity for children to share with each other in the creative process.

(229) 623-5545
www.soundplay.com

WATERPLAY® MANUFACTURING INC.

Kids have always taken to backyard sprinklers, neighborhood fire hydrants and city fountains to cool off. And nothing brings smiles to a park like an exciting world of shapes and showers. Unpredictable sprayers, oversized water cannons and larger than life creatures converge to create spaces dripping with imaginative fun. Happiness reigns over the neighborhood and kids claim their space with an excitement that reminds us of how summer should feel. Leading the transformation of aquatic environments, Waterplay® has turned hundreds of flat concrete slabs into inspiring three dimensional water worlds. Our durable, safe and distinctive creations remain the blueprint for all other imitations.
Make parks fun again. Call us.

(800) 590-5552
www.waterplay.com

ZEAGER

WOODCARPET ® products from Zeager have more to offer. These products include WOODCARPET® engineered wood fiber, DURADRAIN® foam drain that adds fall protection and reduces top off, PVC and foam wear mats that are the most effective at preventing holes and have a no-trip design. WOODCARPET® products are backed by a comprehensive warranty, third-party certifications, and meet ADA, ASTM, CPSC, and CSA playground surfacing standards. Recbase™ is a resilient foam base that provides drainage, fall protection and ease of installation and can be covered with artificial turf, poured in place rubber, or rubber tiles.

(800) 346-8524
www.woodcarpet.com

HOWELL EQUIPMENT

For over 70 years, Howell Equipment has built a reputation for manufacturing and selling durable, long-lasting playground equipment. As a family-owned business, Howell has always understood the value of play. We know that a child's social, mental, and physical development depend on it. It has been proven with a variety of research that play is necessary to promote healthy development of children at all ages and abilities.

A great deal of work and dedication go into our products. We continue to strive to capture the heart of our mission — "It's for the kids!".

(800) 637-5075
www.howellequipment.com

The Beyond Access project emphasizes the inclusion of children with disabilities in public play environments.

Supported by the U.S. Department of Health and Human Services, Administration on Development Disabilities, the Beyond Access project provides technical assistance to both consumers and designers/manufacturers of playground equipment. The project's educational tools focus on ability rather than disability, emphasizing accessibility (physical access) as well as inclusion (social access) that contributes to children's development.

A SALUTE TO BOUNDLESS PLAYGROUNDS' FIRST CORPORATE SPONSOR

Hasbro Boundless Playground
Providence, RI

HASBRO CHILDREN'S FOUNDATION
10 Rockefeller Plaza, 16th Floor, New York, New York 10020
(212) 713-7654

A very special thank you to the extraordinary people at Hasbro for supporting the *National Center for Boundless Playgrounds* for more than 5 years. *Boundless Playgrounds* Hasbro National Resource Center, which was established in 1998 with a significant three-year grant from the Hasbro Children's Foundation, launched *Boundless Playgrounds* outreach and education programs and provided technical assistance to 24 playground projects in economically challenged communities. Hasbro Charitable Trust and Hasbro, Inc. funded *Boundless Playgrounds'* first corporately sponsored public park playground in addition to supporting *Boundless Playgrounds* in so many other ways. *Boundless Playgrounds* would not be where it is today without Hasbro's very generous and ongoing support.

A SALUTE TO LEARNING STRUCTURES & JONATHAN'S DREAM

To celebrate the playground that was the inspiration for Boundless Playgrounds and the team that created it

LEARNING STRUCTURES
144 Back Canaan Road • Strafford, NH 03884
Toll Free: (800) 533-1553
www.learningstructures.com

Learning Structures is the community built playground company that worked with Amy Jaffe Barzach and her family to create Jonathan's Dream in memory of their son Jonathan, who died when he was nine months of age. Learning Structures custom designed each playground structure at this special playground in response to the vision of the Jonathan's Dream committee and created a wonderful playground that could be enjoyed by all. In 1997, inspired by the impact of Jonathan's Dream, Jonathan's mom, Amy Jaffe Barzach (now *Boundless Playgrounds* co-founder and executive director) joined together with Jean Schappet (*Boundless Playgrounds* co-founder and creative director) and a passionate team of parents and professionals to establish the *National Center for Boundless Playgrounds*.

Children Playing at Jonathan's Dream
West Hartford, CT

afterword

THE NATIONAL CENTER FOR BOUNDLESS PLAYGROUNDS® celebrates the publication of this groundbreaking book and its authors Jean Schappet (*Boundless Playgrounds* co-founder and creative director), Antonio Malkusak (*Boundless Playgrounds* director of design) and Lawrence Bruya (charter member of *Boundless Playgrounds* Academic Advisory Board).

The authors of *High Expectations* are available for speaking engagements, keynote addresses and in-house training. Due to demand, availability is limited. Please call 860-243-8315 for more information or to speak to the authors directly.

If you have been inspired by this book, you are invited to visit *Boundless Playgrounds* web site at www.boundless-playgrounds.org. *Boundless Playgrounds* provides leadership, technical support services, programs and training on why and how to create play environments that are barrier-free and developmentally advantageous. *Boundless Playgrounds* is proud to be known as the first national non-profit organization dedicated to playgrounds where children and adults of all abilities can laugh, play, grow and learn together.

Boundless Playgrounds and the authors believe that play environments that give children of all abilities the best opportunities to participate in engaged play have the three essential characteristics described in the table below. When a play environment addresses all three of these characteristics, it can apply for designation as a Boundless Playground®. A playground with one or two of these characteristics can apply for designation as a Playground with Boundless Play Features™. These designations can be awarded by Boundless Playgrounds after a plan review is conducted.

Information on *Boundless Playgrounds* performance standards and rates are available by contacting *Boundless Playgrounds*, 45 Wintonbury Avenue Bloomfield, CT 06002, by calling 860-2433-8315, or by visiting www.boundlessplaygrounds.org.

Essential Characteristics of a Boundless Playground®

Engaged play happens when children...

EXPERIENCE SELF-DIRECTED PLAY

Children of all abilities can discover play elements and configurations that support their predictable play behaviors - every child can find what he/she needs for independent play

EXPERIENCE CHILD-SIZED SPACES

Children of all abilities can experience semi-enclosed spaces - every child can get into child-sized spaces

EXPERIENCE HEIGHT

Children of all abilities can experience height - every child can get to and play on the highest platform centers

The National Center for Boundless Playgrounds® is dedicated to increasing public awareness of the tremendous need for barrier-free and developmentally advantageous playgrounds and to demonstrating how all children, regardless of ability or disability, benefit from them. Established in 1997, *Boundless Playgrounds* was the first national nonprofit organization to provide leadership to foster and create playgrounds where children and adults of all abilities can laugh, play, grow and learn together.

The organization's dramatic growth in 1998 was fueled by a three-year grant from Hasbro Children's Foundation. A four-year grant from the National Football League Charities funded *Boundless Playgrounds* regional initiative strategies in 2001. *Boundless Playgrounds* mission and work were recently recognized by the W.K. Kellogg Foundation with a major grant which launched the Able to Play project that includes the development of up to 20 play environments throughout the state of Michigan, in conjunction with the foundation's 75th anniversary in 2005.

Sixty-three (63) *Boundless Playgrounds* projects are now open in 18 states and Canada. All of these special play environments have been uniquely developed to provide for inclusive play and to remove the barriers that limit childhood exploration and development.

Boundless Playgrounds partners with local and state governments, park departments, schools systems, hospitals, businesses, individuals, children and families, civic organizations, foundations and other nonprofit organizations. *Boundless Playgrounds* offers a wide range of services and technical support to help create these magical places. The goal of the organization is to ultimately have barrier-free and developmentally advantageous playgrounds within reach of every child.

To make a contribution, volunteer, start a project or learn more about *Boundless Playgrounds* programs and services:

Please visit www.boundlessplaygrounds.org or call 860-243-8315.